W9-BTP-770

Gilligan, Maynard & Me

Gilligan, Maynard & Me

Bob Denver

A Citadel Press Book
Published by Carol Publishing Group

Copyright © 1993 by Bob Denver
All rights reserved. No part of this book may be reproduced in any
form, except by a newspaper or magazine reviewer who wishes to
quote brief passages in connection with a review.

A Citadel Press Book
Published by Carol Publishing Group
Citadel Press is a registered trademark of Carol
Communications, Inc.
Editorial Offices: 600 Madison Avenue, New York, N.Y. 10022
Sales & Distribution Offices: 120 Enterprise Avenue, Secaucus,
   N.J. 07094
In Canada: Canadian Manda Group, P.O. Box 920, Station U,
   Toronto, Ontario M8Z 5P9
Queries regarding rights and permissions should be addressed to
Carol Publishing Group, 600 Madison Avenue, New York, N.Y. 10022

Carol Publishing Group books are available at special discounts
for bulk purchases, for sales promotions, fund-raising, or
educational purposes. Special editions can be created to specifications.
For details, contact: Special Sales Department, Carol Publishing
Group, 120 Enterprise Avenue, Secaucus, N.J. 07094

Manufactured in the United States of America
10 9 8 7 6 5 4 3 2 1

Designed by Paul and Dolores Gamarello/Eyetooth Design Inc.

Library of Congress Cataloging-in-Publication Data
Denver, Bob.
    Gilligan, Maynard, and me / by Bob Denver.
       p. cm.
    "A Citadel Press book."
    ISBN 0-8065-1413-2 (paper)
    1. Denver, Bob. 2. Gilligan's Island (Television program)
3. Many loves of Dobie Gillis (Television program) I. Title.
PN1992.77.G53D46 1993
791.45'028'092—dc20   92-37556
[B]   CIP

TO
DREAMS

CONTENTS

ot to live out my fantasy on *Fantasy Island* as
perhero "Eagleman." Get me back to *Gilligan's*
nd.

PREFACE

I've been Gilligan for almost thirty years. People are always asking me, "Does it bother you?" Absolutely not. The only thing that is annoying is that none of the cast (of castaways) makes any money from the reruns. We were paid off in two years! But in 1963, no one could foresee the syndication market. By the early eighties, I estimated that the show had grossed over a billion dollars, and it keeps rolling on. But the past is the past, and you let it go. (But boy could I use a billion dollars!) Seriously, the fans more than make up for the loss of the money. In all the years it's been on, no one has come up to me with anything less than a big grin and a thank-you. It makes me feel good. The fans have always been the same—the only slight change being after twenty years, the ones in their seventies and eighties wanted the autograph for themselves, instead of for their kids or grandchildren. They remember when they were in their fifties and were really poppin'. The majority, though, watched as children and grew up with it. More than anything else I guess I hear, "I ran home from school every day and turned it on!" I've found that being a good childhood memory is very rewarding.

In the last six years, the *Dobie Gillis* series has been running on Nickelodeon. Maynard G. Krebs fans are coming on strong. They're very loyal. When I ask them what they think of Gilligan, they say, "He's okay, but Maynard is my man." When they were turning thirty, they would come up and whisper in my ear that they watched the show. Now their children's children are watching the reruns. I can see them trying to explain what a beatnik is. Good luck.

This book is for all of you who have fond memories of these shows. Keep watching and enjoying. I had great fun doing them.

happy, post-Gilligan mood on the set
he *Good Guys*.

LIFE BEFORE TELEVISION

I was bitten by the acting bug when, against my will and all I held dear, I was forced onstage. When I made my entrance, the audience burst into laughter. I hadn't even said a word. I was a sophomore at Loyola University in Los Angeles. The speech teacher who ran the drama department asked me to be the house manager for the little theater on campus. Little it was. It sat ninety people and had formerly been a chapel.

Now, *house manager* was a fancy title for janitor, though I did hand out programs and help build sets. I was perfectly happy. At the start of my junior year the speech teacher, who of course directed all the plays, wanted me to read for a part. It was the comedy relief in the play *The Caine Mutiny Court-Martial*. I said absolutely not. It was pure agony just to give a speech in class. There was no way I was going to stand onstage in a play. Just thinking about it gave me the shakes. I mean, I had done some offstage lines in the greenroom the year before, and that had terrified me. An actor I was not.

"Just read for the part," they kept saying. "It doesn't mean you're going to get it." On the night of the reading they got me to show up on some pretext, and since I was there, why not read? The part called for an extremely nervous young seaman testifying at the court-martial. They wouldn't let up, so I finally read. Just to get it over with. In almost a whisper, mumbling and stuttering and at the speed of light, I did it. It had to be the worst reading in the history of theater. I got the part.

We started rehearsals. My reading was proving to be prophetic: there was no improvement onstage. The director tried everything. I had memorized the scene—there were not that many lines. I would be "out there" less than five minutes, but I knew I wouldn't be there on opening night. I'd have a nervous breakdown way before that, the flu would attack me, something would happen. Nothing did. Opening night arrived.

The theater was at the end of a dormitory. The bathroom was at the end of a long hallway, past all the students' rooms. Two hours before curtain, I sauntered down to the bathroom and threw up. I'd never been that nervous. I don't know how many trips I made down that hall, but some of the students in the rooms along the way started noticing me. They shouted out encouraging words like, "You'll never make it onstage!" "Anybody keeping count? I've got a dollar riding on the number eight!" The curtain went up, and since I didn't appear until late in the play, I thought I could make one more trip. I couldn't move, much less walk. I sat in the greenroom frozen. Someone got me up and led me by the arm to the door for my entrance. I was shaking, sweating, and numb. This couldn't be happening. My cue came and I stepped onstage. I heard the laugh and the rest is a blur. Like all actors starting out, all I wanted was to get off that stage. I did my lines, heard some more laughs, and escaped. It was over, thank God, never again. The next night, there I was, in the same shape doing it again. I don't know how many performances there were, but the conventional wisdom is that it gets easier the more you do it. What isn't mentioned is that for some actors that means years, not a few times. Still, those ninety people laughing their heads off fascinated me. After all, what they saw was a shaking sailor who was petrified at being in court. It was just me reacting to being onstage. Not much acting, but it fit the part perfectly. As the run went on, I could gradually hear the other actors and actually remember some of what happened out there. When it was over, I knew acting wasn't for me. Who would put up with such torture voluntarily? So when they asked me to do the next play, I said yes.

In my senior year, having five productions under my belt, I felt ready to tackle Shakespeare. Not only to speak the words trippingly off my tongue, but to play Falstaff in *Henry the Fourth, Part Two*. The only excuse for this behavior is youth and no perspective. Falstaff is a character in his fifties and weighs two hundred and fifty pounds. He's fat. I looked sixteen years old and was skinny. I hid behind makeup and the Elizabethan costume. Boots up to midthigh, tunic over the top of the boots. The bird legs didn't show. Big lacy cuffs flopping over the hands so only the fingertips peeked out. A false stomach, with a pillow behind it, strapped on. A floppy hat, with feather, draped over the face. A wig, a beard, and large false eyebrows completed the deception. The only thing that really showed were my eyes. Believe me, with all that stuff on, I sweated like a fat man. What saved the show was an actor born to do Shakespeare. He was fantastic. When he was onstage emoting, the audience was mesmerized. Still, doing that play taught me a lot. Especially about limitations. We fenced all over the campus, this being one of the main reasons we wanted to do Shakespeare. We were dueling in front of the administration building when the head man came out and said if he saw us with foils in our hands one more time, whacking away at each other, he would cancel us.

Of course college was more than just acting. By the start of my sophomore year, I was asking those big questions like, "Where am I going?" "Why am I still in school?" "Why is the world in such a mess?" The Russians had invaded Hungary and I joined a group of students who thought it was outrageous. We made our own placards and marched in protest around City Hall, in downtown L.A. I was at loose ends and decided to quit school. That semester my grades plunged to straight Ds. I wanted out.

What I had forgotten was the army was waiting for me. I was on a student deferment. When I came to my senses, I asked the university for a second chance and was put on probation. It was the next semester that I joined the acting group. I also got off probation. Maybe acting kept me out of the army.

Or maybe it was the fact that I broke my neck. I was driving to the university to do a play. I had borrowed my dad's tux to use as a costume, and it was in the backseat. I had been sworn to take care of it, and I made a turn and heard it sliding off the seat. I turned around to catch it and went into a parked car. A big old Cadillac. I was driving a small English sedan, a Humber Hawk. The Cadillac's bumper was bent; my car was totaled. The Humber had been in cherry condition, too.

When not acting or going to school, I had a string of odd jobs. One summer, my brother, Richard, and I worked at Yellowstone Park. I worked at the grocery store, across from Old Faithful. Every day at least ten people asked when it was going to go off. When I couldn't take any more, I told them, "I'll go and ask the park ranger when he's going to turn it on."

I had worked at different manufacturing plants around L.A. since I had been in high school. Day shift, swing shift when I started to do plays. I had one job where I acquired an assistant. This was unusual, because as temporary help, I always had a job on the lower end of ability. Why train someone who was going to leave in three months? This job required me to stand in front of a machine that I think was invented by Rube Goldberg. All it did was flare one end of copper tubing, ten inches by one-quarter inch. You loaded a handful of the tubing at the top, and they came down to a clockwork thing, which passed them over some gas jets. The jets heated one end and then dropped them down so the end could be flared. The machine was taller than me. It made a *ching ching* sound as it worked. All I had to do was load the top and empty the bottom. Eight hours of this made you a little loony. Then one shift a guy came by and asked why I never called him. He said he repaired the machines when they broke down. I told him that this machine hadn't shown the slightest inclination of breaking down. He carefully looked around, then took one of the copper tubes and jammed it in the clockwork gears. The machine shuddered to a stop. He told me then to turn off the gas and push that button over there. A red light would go on summoning him. I had always wondered what that button did. So, when I was at wit's end, I did as he asked. That's why an assistant was redundant, unless his task was to push the button.

The man who was assigned as my assistant was in his sixties and was part-time, too. Now what was this guy doing working in a factory at his age? The noise of the machine prevented any conversation, and I didn't know what to say to him anyway. We just stood there and watched the machine. It took all of a minute to show him what to do. We split the job. I loaded, he unloaded. By this time I'd found an old wooden box to sit on and got him one. We sat. A couple of days went by and I still didn't know what to make of him. Then he shouted above the noise, "The sound of the machine reminds me of the camels' bells in the Sahara Desert!" They were the first words he had spoken. I thought, "Uh-oh, I've got me a crazy," and looked for a fast exit. I was a little scared, too. It turned out he was a full professor of ancient history and had arrived too late in this country to land a teaching position at the college of his choice. It was one of the best summers I spent working. I was even a little sorry to see it end. We talked, or rather, he lectured all that summer. He told me of his extensive travels and taught me ancient history. Every time I hear anything that remotely sounds like *ching ching*, it all comes back to me.

After I graduated I was a little lost. I read all the books that I hadn't the time for when in college and sat on my duff. I was trying to make up my mind whether to become a lawyer or an actor. My brother had just finished the first year of law school. This meant that I would get all his books free and a tutor, too. Being a lawyer meant financial security, a safe life. Being an actor meant just the opposite. As September grew closer, I still hadn't made up my mind. I knew this was to be one of the bigger decisions of my life. What it came down to was which one I'd be happiest doing. I chose acting. It fascinated me. Making people laugh seemed better than getting mixed up with the law. Easier said than done. I had to get a job to support myself.

The local parochial grammar school, Corpus Christi in Pacific Palisades, was looking for a coach and part-time teacher. The coaching job involved—what else?—coaching the seventh- and eighth-graders in sports so the school could join an intramural league. It also entailed taking out all grades for recess. I took it. It paid just enough to get by on, and I knew I could work at the post office to take up the slack.

I showed up on the first day of school decked out in what I thought a coach should wear. A sweatshirt, whistle around my neck, and a clipboard. I got the first-graders for recess. This was in '57. It was baby boomer time. There were two first-grade classrooms. Forty-two little boys poured out. I was prepared; they weren't. It was the first day of school for them, too. They milled around aimlessly while I told them who I was and that they had to get in a line to go to the playground. The only reaction I received was scared looks. I told them to line up again in a stern coach's voice. They were really frightened then. I blew my whistle. Wrong thing to do. I think they would have all run home if they had known the way. I finally took the least petrified one by the arm and told him to stand still, don't move. I grabbed another and put him behind the first and so on. It didn't take long for it to become clear that a single line of forty-two six-year-olds is not workable. By twos was the answer. The only problem with this was, by the time I was putting couple sixteen in place, the whole front of the line had wandered away. I was sweating; they were cool. Time passed. Then persistence paid off. There was the line. Perfect. Well, maybe a little wavery, and then a bell went off. End of recess. They went back into their classrooms exhausted but happy. What did they know? Recess could be learning how to line up and watching that grown-up running around like a nut.

I was watching the sixth grade play baseball when I realized nothing really changes. The captains chose their teams, picking the boys who played poorly last. What embarrassment. They always struck out. It was expected of them. The time of play was torture. So, I changed the rules of the game. There would be no foul lines. The good players were confused. The bad ones got the idea right away. If you could just get your bat to touch the ball, it was a hit. For the first time in their lives they were running the bases. One turned and hit the ball at the catcher. Nobody wanted to play that position after that. It was a circus. When somebody fouled a ball, all the good players yelled, "Foul ball!" Meanwhile, the hitter was rounding first, heading for second. But all good things come to an end. They wanted rules. I think they needed them. Back to regular baseball. Still, every once in a while, I'd throw in a no-rules game.

In the summer, one of the teachers ran a day camp at the school. I changed titles: *coach* to *counselor*. It was an easy transition. The kids loved that day camp. Organized activities were minimal. A lot of free play. Counselors bombing each other with water balloons.

I had gone to a day camp when I was nine. It was nothing like this one. I remember being in a skit about Snow White and the seven dwarfs. One guess which dwarf I played. Yup, Dopey. I wore a yellow raincoat and dwarf hat. No lines, just marching around in a circle. The people laughed at me. They thought I was the perfect Dopey. Maybe *that* was the start of my acting career. It was certainly a solid basis for Maynard and especially Gilligan.

It was during the second teaching year that I got the call to be Maynard.

MY BIG BREAK

Once in a while someone asks how I got started in TV. The answer I give is that it's really all luck, being in the right place at the right time. Other actors say the same thing. It's all in the timing. In my case, I was asleep on the couch when the call came from Twentieth Century-Fox! The studio! Talk about being in the right place at the right time. I shouldn't have been at home in my mother's house on a Friday afternoon in December at around four P.M. I should have been at the local post office, where I had a part-time job. I worked in the early morning and late at night. In between, from nine to three, I was teaching at a local grammar school. I was beat and I couldn't see myself sorting mail, so I came home and collapsed on the couch.

The phone must have rung at least ten times before I staggered over and answered it. The secretary said that a producer was interviewing young actors for a possible screen test for a part in a pilot. Somehow I had got on that list of actors. Actually, my sister, Helen, was working at the studio and slipped my name in. I found out later that the producer had already interviewed close to a thousand actors. I really didn't feel like going all the way over to Twentieth to sit and talk about myself. I had been going out to these interviews for about two years already, and I thought they were a waste of time. Always the same questions:

STUDIO BIGWIG: What credits do you have?

ME: None.

SB: Do you have any film I could look at?

ME: No.

SB: Do you have an agent?

ME: No, they want film, too.

bie and Maynard, buddies forever.
holes in *this* sweatshirt.

Loyola University of Los Angeles

presents

The Del Rey Players

in

THE CAINE MUTINY COURT-MARTIAL

by

Herman Wouk

directed by

Paul Blackburn

SB: Well, what experience do you have?

ME: In college I did Shakespeare, and after that, plays around the city.

SB: Hmmm. Okay. The next time you're in a play, call the office and I'll try to get down and see it. Thanks for coming in. Next!

ME: (*aside*) The only way to get a casting person to really come and see you in a play is to get a hammerlock on them and drag them physically to the theater. Not recommended.

Then I asked the secretary, "Would I get a drive-on pass?" This was a big deal, because then you could pretend you were working at the studio, and if you were careful, you could even sneak over to the back lot and look around. There were acres and acres of back lot filled with unbelievable sets. There was a full-sized Moorish castle, a twelfth-century French village, a jungle, a western town, a lake and stream, all kinds of good stuff. Years later, I used to go and have picnics there. Ah, the rewards of stardom. Anyway, the secretary said yes, and so I went to the interview.

The producer said I was too old to play a high school student. He said I certainly looked young enough, around eighteen, but at the ripe old age of twenty-three, I was too old. Made sense. But if I showed up Monday at the stage where they were shooting the tests, he would interview me on camera. He would ask me my name, where I lived, and all that jazz, and then he would give me the film. I think he felt sorry for me, but who cared? Now I could answer the question "You have any film?" I might even be able to get an agent.

That weekend I got a haircut and slept as much as I could, hoping I would look younger. I know he said I was too old, but maybe Monday he would look at me and say, "My God! You look five years younger!" That would make me look thirteen, but who knows, maybe they would test me. I had no idea what a screen test consisted of, but I would be ready.

On Monday, I drove on the lot again and went to the soundstage where the tests were being filmed. This time I was dressed like my students.

I stood around soaking up the atmosphere. I was on a real live soundstage

The Caine Mutiny Court-Martial may h made me nauseous, but it was the beginn of my acting car

10

and I was going to stand in front of a real camera! Pretty hot stuff. Nobody knew why I was there. The director called the producer's office, but he wasn't there and they didn't know how to reach him. The director kept asking me, "Why are you here?" I mumbled something. "Who are you?" I mumbled some more. "Are you here to test?" My heart leaped. I said, "The producer said for me to show up." He said, "Well, where's your copy of the test scene?" I gave him the best blank look I could muster. He looked at me like I was an idiot. "Jeez, this kid might be perfect as Maynard." He handed me the test scene and said, "Can you memorize this?" It was five pages of dialogue with Dobie. "Sure," I said, and stood there looking at it. "Not here," he yelled. "Go in that dressing room over there with the script girl and she'll run the lines with you. And hurry up, you're the last person to be tested!"

I looked around for the script girl, but the only person waving to me was a lady in her sixties. I went to her and she took my hand and we went into the dressing room. I could still hear the director yelling, "How many have we tested? A hundred? And on the last day this has to happen? Okay, everybody relax for thirty minutes and then get that kid into wardrobe and stick on the goatee."

I sat with the woman in a canvas knockdown dressing room and started trying to learn the test scene. I could hear the crew setting up. I was the last actor to be tested, and they'd been doing this for weeks. They wanted to go home. The wardrobe man brought in a ratty pair of sneakers, a pair of chino pants, and a gray sweatshirt full of holes.

We ran the lines for about twenty minutes, and then the script girl said I'd have a chance to do the scene a couple of times when we blocked it for the cameras. The makeup man stuck his head in the door and said, "Come on, kid, time to get made up." As he was gluing the goatee on, I thought, "First time in front of the cameras, I'll just forget they're there and act like I'm onstage." Like I had a choice.

I went to the set, met Dwayne Hickman, and shook hands. We had a nodding acquaintance because we had attended Loyola University at the same time. The director said, "Let's get this over with!" We rehearsed the scene and ran the lines. This was the first time I heard the time-honored routine: "Put it on a bell." A bell went off like a school fire alarm. "Quiet on the set!" Then, "Roll 'em!" Then a voice in the distance: "Speed." Then, "Marker," and there in front of me was the man with the slate; he slammed the markers together with a whack and then came the fabled "Action!" Dwayne and I did the scene. He was great. I don't know how many times he had had to do this scene during the weeks and weeks of testing, but he was there for me. Lots of energy and real smooth. Thanks, Dwayne. Suddenly, it was over and the first

One of the cardinal rules of acting is never do scenes with kids or animals. It's one rule I never learned.

assistant director shouted, "That's a wrap," and everybody was gone and I was sitting in the dressing room. The goatee was gone, so was the sweatshirt, and I thought, "Well, I've got some film at last, now I can get an agent." I've heard recently that someone at Fox came across the test scene in its archives. I'd dearly love to see it.

Weeks went by and I didn't hear from the studio. I didn't really expect anything; after all, they'd tested over a hundred actors. Then in January the producer's secretary called and said I was up for the part of Maynard with fifty other guys. I wasn't too excited. Then she called and said it was between one other actor and me, and would I be available to shoot the pilot? I got excited. A pilot! A whole half hour of film. Much better than just a scene. It still hadn't registered that there might be a series. The final call came. I had the part and the script was being mailed to me. The pilot was going to shoot in two weeks.

THE MAKING OF MAYNARD

The script for the *Dobie Gillis* pilot arrived in mid-'58, and I sat right down and read it. In the story Dobie falls for Thalia Menninger (Tuesday Weld), a delectable mercenary. No money, no Thalia. There's a weekly jackpot drawing at the local cinema, and Dobie, with Maynard's help, is going to rig it so he wins. His conscience overcomes him, and he fails to collect on the winning ticket. He finds out later, of course, that he had won legitimately.

After I finished reading the script, Dobie and Maynard's relationship became clear. They were good friends. Dobie suffered Maynard because Maynard's heart was in the right place and he'd do anything for Dobie. Also, Dobie was the only person Maynard had in his life. He was also a bona fide beatnik and jazz fanatic. This was the late fifties and beatniks were the funkiest things around.

I had been to coffeehouses in L.A. where beatniks hung out, and they fascinated me. I listened to their beat poetry and jargon. I even tried to wade my way through the beats' bible, *On the Road* by Jack Kerouac. During the first year of playing Maynard, I was allowed to make up my character. Not too many of the writers knew what a beatnik was like. When you start a series, all you have to go on is one script and a vague idea of who you're playing. As the series progresses, little pieces of the person become known. I'd been lucky enough to play a beatnik in college in a production of Gilbert and Sullivan's *Patience*. You might wonder how beatniks got into Gilbert and Sullivan. We changed the two opposing factions to advertising men in suits against beatniks. In college productions you can get away with anything.

So when I got to play a beatnik, I made sure he was a real protest cat . . . man. I tried to put the word *like* in every sentence Maynard uttered. Also *man* and *cool*. Usually together. Every once in a while I would throw in a tangled cliché like "Starve a cold, feed a fever" just to keep everyone confused.

Maynard was also a jazz fan. I mean, like, he was obsessed, man. If he hadn't had Dobie for a friend, he would have stayed in his room all the time just listening to jazz. He was a fun person to play. I liked him. I wasn't certain how the parents of America were going to react. In those days there were only the three networks and maybe an independent station in the large cities. TV was still a novelty. Everybody watched and talked about what they had seen the night before. I tried to imagine the audience I was reaching. Millions didn't compute.

Playing a character like Maynard was an actor's dream come true. He was mine to create. Sounds a bit like Dr. Frankenstein, but it was true. There was no stereotype to base the character on, like the "boy next door" or "typical teenager." Also, I was into jazz. Just like Maynard, I dug Thelonius Monk and Dizzy Gillespie. Sometimes you get real lucky.

My memories of shooting the pilot are still kind of murky. I saw it on cable TV not too long ago. My strongest memories are of the dream sequence in which Dobie and I are dressed up as thirties gangsters. We are holding off the cops in a cheap hotel room. While shooting the scene, a crew member came on the set and started putting these little red pellets, attached to real thin wire, all over the hotel room. On the walls, the lamps, the windows, everywhere. He came over to me and said, "Ya see where they all are? Okay? Ya know what to do?" I nodded, not having a clue. I asked another crew member what those little red things were, and he said, "Squibs. They make bullet holes, stay away from them." How? They were all over the place. I also didn't know how loud they were. The set was built on a platform ten feet up. There was one camera on the floor outside, aimed up at the room, and they said they could see there was no ceiling. So a ceiling was tacked on. I was now in a box with just one opening. We shot the scene, always stopping when I went to the window to break it and fire my pistol. This was the cue for the squibs. When they went off, I never did know what I did until I saw the film. I had run into a corner of the room with my hands over my ears and froze there. I didn't hear "Cut!" I didn't hear anything for ten minutes. I learned then and there, always ask the effects man to explain everything. In fact, after that, special effects became my favorite department at the studio.

When the week of shooting the pilot was over, I went back to my normal routine of teaching and working at the post office. The money for the pilot was minimal, and the bills didn't stop coming in. The kids at the school weren't impressed that I had a foot in the door of show biz. They were worried that I might have to leave them to do a series. When it happened, they were very

Here I am playing the bongo for Dobie in full b
regalia. You can almost see my na

distressed: "Mr. Denver! How can you leave us for a TV show!" They never really forgave me. Years later, whenever I'd run into one of my students, they'd still be pissed off. Recently, I got a letter from one of the more rowdy boys. He's been a pilot for Delta the last seventeen years. He hoped that I would mention the "unruly surfer dudes from the Pacific Palisades who were blown away by your classroom departure." He signed the letter, "Your 8th Grade Little Buddy." Well, he got his wish.

After the pilot was shot, I asked if I could follow it through its various postproduction departments until it was ready. The studio said okay and looked at me like I'd lost my mind. I went to editing and watched the cutter put pieces of film together, and then I went to the music department and learned that Lionel Newman was going to score it. Even I knew of him. He had been head of the music department for years at Twentieth Century-Fox, with major movies to his credit. He was an Academy Award winner. I thought that he would take some canned music and add it to the pilot. Nope. When I went to the music department, they sent me to the scoring stage, and there was Mr. Newman with a full orchestra. I watched how he put his original music to each scene. This dinky little half-hour show was getting the full treatment! Music to open the scene with the right mood. Music to close the scene. He was there all day, stopping and starting, until he was satisfied. He was the first person to tell me that the best music was the kind you didn't hear at first. It should put you in the mood without you noticing. He had written the theme song and all the music for the show, even adding a musical sting when Maynard appeared. All this for a little half-hour pilot. But this was when Twentieth was still acting like a major studio. They don't exist anymore.

In fact, I signed a seven-year contract with the studio after the pilot sold, a dream come true. Max Shulman saw me right after I signed. I was walking down the street on the lot by his office when he came out and asked if I had a contract yet. Proudly, I answered, "Yes! A studio contract!" He said, "You schmuck! You should have signed a five-year TV deal. You're going to be working at least forty weeks on the series. Who's your agent!" I said, "I don't have one." "Figures," he said, and went back in his office. My very first negotiation and I'd goofed. It wasn't to be the last time.

The pilot sold and we started shooting the series in February of '59 for the fall debut. I said good-bye to my students and, with great joy, quit the post office. TV was a still a new medium, and I had no idea that I would spend the next eleven years of my life immersed in it. That first year we shot thirty-nine episodes. I missed one. I was drafted after the fourth.

When I graduated from college, the draft board called me in and said that my student deferment was over and I was now eligible for the draft. I had two

GI blues. Only breaking my neck kept m
of the real

years of army ROTC in high school and two years of air force ROTC in college, and I must say the military didn't seem to be my cup of tea. At the meeting, I told them that I was the sole support of my mother, but they kept insinuating I was lying, and I, of course, lost my temper. I called the head of the draft board a pragmatist. I could tell he thought it was a dirty word. The studio tried to get me deferred and used an ex-army general to pull some strings. Everything was okay until it reached the local level. There the head man always screamed, "Draft him!" So much for using big words. I reported to a building in down-town L.A. for my physical, and as I waited in one of the numerous lines, I read in the *L.A. Times* that I was being drafted and had lost the part of Maynard. A very low point in my life. An actor named Michael J. Pollard had been hired to play the part. Talk about being depressed. Anyway, I didn't pass the physical. I'd broken my neck in '56, and when I came to the tiny space on the medical form that said, "State your present health," I filled it up with five lines of symptoms about my neck. It got me out of line, a couple of X rays, and a sarge who said I wasn't eligible. I got out of that building in record time and ran down the street leaping and shouting.

I went back to the set and told the producers the army didn't want me. They weren't too happy. Michael J. Pollard had been signed for thirty episodes and had only done one. They told me to go home and they would call me. Those three days were long. The call finally came. I was back in the series and Michael was paid off. I heard later he said that he had heard of coming to California to discover gold, but hadn't believed it until now.

In the fourth Dobie Gillis episode Maynard got drafted just like I did, so I waited to see how Max would get him out. Dobie asked Maynard, what happened? Maynard said he'd gotten a hardship discharge. For who? The army. End of scene. That was the way Max wrote.

We previewed the first thirteen episodes to live audiences so their laughs could be recorded. The laugh track was sweetened later by a man who had a machine with every kind of laugh imaginable in it. They were in a large black case, about the size of a suitcase. It had a small keyboard that he played like a piano. He was truly a virtuoso of giggles and guffaws. In the early years of television, the laugh-track man was a deep, dark secret. No one admitted he existed. He did his work at night, after everyone went home. I met him during *Gilligan*, after he was allowed to come out of the laugh closet. He was incredible. Over the years he had recorded on tape or taken from tape laughs from the radio days or from live performances. He edited them until he and only he knew where they were. The machine was like a tape recorder from *Star Wars*. With his left hand he could produce belly laughs, while his right hand brought in light laughter fading into applause. With him working on a show it was possible to get a laugh with a simple hello. He was discerning though. He would watch a show at least three times, laughing out loud to himself, then put the laughs in where he thought it was funny. He had job security since he was the only one who had the machine. Still, think of all the TV shows he worked on that were not funny. What a way to make a living! The only answer is, he must have been an artist. He was creating something out of nothing. I sometimes wonder if he was laughing at the absurdity of it all.

DOBIE GILLIS FOR PRESIDENT

BACKSTAGE ON THE
DOBIE GILLIS SHOW

Max Shulman was the creator, head writer, and producer of the *The Many Loves of Dobie Gillis*. I had read all of his books and felt lucky to be working for him. As a writer of fiction he had a long list of bestsellers, including *Barefoot Boy With Cheek* and *Rally 'Round the Flag, Boys* which was made into a successful movie. He had an off-center sense of humor that appealed to me. He liked attacking sacred cows and really had a feeling for the absurd. Take the G. in Maynard G. Krebs. It appeared out of nowhere and I said it for a couple episodes before I asked Max what it stood for. He said, "Walter," and the next script explained it. Maynard was named after his aunt Walter, who was married to Uncle Ethel. Another time, I asked him why the Maynard character wasn't in the original Dobie Gillis books. He said because he wanted to sell a few copies.

Then there was the case of the disappearing holes in my sweatshirt. When I started, the shirt had holes everywhere. The one that bothered me the most was situated on the right side of my chest. If I didn't wear a T-shirt underneath, my nipple peeked out. It was very disconcerting. I told the wardrobe man we had to do something about it. He said that the producers wanted nothing to be changed. Since he was the one that cut the holes in the sweatshirt, I suggested that each week he make the holes a little smaller in the most embarrassing places. That way they would slowly disappear and nobody would notice. I'd wear the sweatshirt with just a few holes in some episodes to establish it; then they couldn't change it back. It worked. Over seven or eight shows the holes slowly faded. I'd been wearing the "new" sweatshirt for three episodes when Max noticed. "Hey, Denver, you have on the wrong sweatshirt. Get it off!" I explained what had transpired and he grinned and

said kids weren't into politics in the late fifties?

said, "Good thinking, but I'm going to be watching you real close from now on."

I always thought that the series was a burlesque of the American family: a son whose whole life was chasing girls, a father who was going to kill him one day, a mother who was too sweet and good to be real, and a best friend who was the only beatnik in a ten-state area.

We shot 142 episodes in four years. Max was there for the first two seasons and came back for the fourth. I think he "went Hollywood" during the third. It happens to the best of them. It kind of creeps up on you. You're working long hours and your private life goes to hell. You're surrounded by people who almost always say yes to anything, tell you how great you are and how you're the boss. It's very easy to "go Hollywood." Max wasn't the first and I certainly wasn't the last. It's like tunnel vision run by an overheated superego.

Max hired various other writers to do scripts, but they were never as good as his own. In the fourth year I read a script that seemed pretty familiar. It was. Max had found an obscure Writers Guild ruling that allowed him to submit the same script if 40 percent was changed. He had his secretary count all the words in a script from the first season and changed exactly 40 percent. I asked him why, and he said his secretary didn't have enough to do. This was before computers, too! I miss Max.

We had one writer who was obsessed with making changes. He was incapable of leaving a script alone. We called him Blue Page. On Monday we would read through the script, all white pages, and on Tuesday here came all the blue pages. The changes in a script proceed in colored pages. After blue came pink, then green, yellow, purple, etc. By the time Blue Page was done he had invented colors never before seen in motion pictures or TV. No one could keep up, but nothing stopped Blue Page. I asked Max why (would I never learn) and he said, "It makes for a pretty script."

All of this made me realize that writing a half-hour script was a gift. Try to tell a story in twenty-two minutes with two long interruptions and not lose your audience. Not easy to do. Also, it has to be funny. I think the best form is a teaser, two acts, and a tag. Critics are always saying that TV stinks. Almost all the sitcoms are dumb, not funny, not interesting. They should sit down and try to write. Anything. Much less a sitcom. It wouldn't take too long for them to realize that good writers work longer hours than anyone else, and that writing a half-hour TV comedy seems to be a God-given gift. In my career I've been blessed with two such writers, Max and Sherwood Schwartz, who wrote *Gilligan*. Not only did they write original scripts, they polished other writers' scripts, were in charge of casting all the actors, and as executive producers had to deal with the network. It was during *Gilligan* when it dawned on me

what went into making a sitcom. Sherwood was kind enough to let me see behind the scenes. What a mess! It made me very grateful that all I had to do was show up and act. Writers work in offices, and when I started, I worked on a soundstage and had enough trouble trying to figure out what was going on around me.

In the old days, the crew consisted of fifty or sixty men and one woman, who were all around me on the stage. It looked like complete pandemonium, but of course it wasn't. Everybody was divided into departments. Camera, electric, laborers, props, and special effects. When I finally understood it all, I was still amazed. A good crew adds immeasurably to the success of a show. When you're working ten or twelve hours a day together, a bond develops. I remember many times a crew member coming up to me with a suggestion to make a scene funnier. After all, some of those guys had been watching actors for thirty or forty years. I always tried what they offered and told them, "If it works, it's my idea, if it doesn't, it's your idea."

Our director of photography, a veteran from the thirties, ran the set. He never cut a scene by speaking out loud. He'd take his cigar wrapper and crinkle it up. The soundman would yell cut. The man who lit the set had a trick I've never seen again, anywhere. He would get behind you, tap your foot, and by the time you looked down and turned around, he'd be two giant steps away, holding up his light meter and yelling to a man on the catwalk to adjust a light. There was no way you could believe he had anything to do with the thump on your foot. He did it to a young actress until she thought she had lost her mind. Then he asked her what was wrong. She told him and he said it was caused by the cables on the floor. The electric current in them. Don't step on them. Naturally, at the end of one of her scenes she was surrounded by cables and he graciously offered to carry her over them.

The set got hotter and hotter as the day went on. The countertops could almost burn your hand. The set was lighted so there wouldn't be shadows. Anywhere. There were lights up high, all over the floor, and hanging from the catwalks were something called pans. This was a huge round light and there were four of them. I never saw them used again. Either because they were old-fashioned or some actor died from heat prostration. You could cause a shadow, though, by leaning the wrong way in a scene. When there are two actors in a scene, each one has a key light. When I first heard the head cameraman yell at me to "clear my light," I just stood there like a dummy. He came over and took me by the shoulders and pointed up at a light. "That one is yours, and that one over there is the other actor's." I looked up and there were lights everywhere, but I found the one shining directly on me. I took a step so I was in it. "No, stay on your mark and just lean a little to clear your light," he said. When I did that, a dark shadow fell on the other actor. He said, "Now, you're in his light. Rock back and clear his light." I did that and lost sight of my light. Staying on my mark, I leaned back, forward, sideways. I rock-and-rolled until I found the sweet spot. I thought, "Let's see now. I enter on action and find my mark, without looking at it, clear my light, and make sure I'm not in the other actor's light. What else? Oh, yeah, do my lines."

Hitting your mark, without looking for it, is not as easy as it sounds. Especially when you're walking, talking, and chewing gum at the same time. A mark is just that. A chalk *T* on the floor. Your feet fit in the *T* or you are not in the frame of the camera. If you miss your mark, the camera operator then clicks off the camera and shakes his head. The director asks what's wrong, and the operator quietly tells him. Depending on who the director is, it is either a big deal or just take two.

We had one director on *Dobie* who embarrassed all of us. I don't think it's necessary to name him. A young, inexperienced actress missed her mark by a mile. I don't think she even knew what it was. She was very nervous, and I'm sure it was her first time in front of the cameras. She was concentrating on the words, hoping she wouldn't forget them. The cameraman went to her and showed her the mark and told her to just stop there and do her lines. The director glowered at her. The second take was worse than the first. The director started yelling at her. She started to tremble. It went on, take after take. She was close to tears. Finally, the director grabbed a hammer, nails, and some short pieces of two-by-fours. He was screaming at her as he hammered together a T. "Let's see you miss this!" he said. She burst into tears and we had to shut down for twenty minutes. His cruel and unnecessary behavior made me lose any respect I had for him. While we waited for her to get herself together, a crew member removed the wooden T. We all sat there staring at the floor. It was very quiet. She came back, did the scene, hitting her mark, and left. It wasn't the only time I'd see a director think he was God.

Since I was brand-new to working on a set, I was open to all the practical jokes. Dobie and Maynard are in a dream sequence in a barren desert, dying of thirst. Maynard drinks the last of the water from the canteen. I could smell the straight Scotch coming. I held it in my mouth, faked swallowing, spit it back, and finished the scene. The set went dark and the crew moved to another part of the stage. I hid behind a sand dune and waited. Here came the propman, Joe, and his assistant whispering to themselves. "I know it was in there!" "Maybe somebody switched the canteen." The assistant picked up the canteen, uncapped it, and I leaped out shouting, "Gotcha!" He jumped and sprayed his partner with the Scotch. Most of that day I'd walk by Joe and say he shouldn't be drinking on the job.

Yvonne Lime as one of the many elu
loves in Dobie's

Another time, Maynard leaps into a large indoor pool with a paddle and is supposed to gleefully enjoy himself. We were to shoot at ten-thirty in the morning, but it kept getting moved back: before lunch, right after lunch. Finally at four, we moved to another stage where the pool was set up. All day, I'd tried to get to see it so I could kind of rehearse. Never made it. I was always stopped, and even though I was slightly suspicious, I couldn't think of what they could do to a pool. We arrived and suddenly we were behind schedule. Quick, jump in! I did. They had been putting ice cubes in the pool all morning and had to wait for them to melt. That's why we had to wait to shoot the scene. When I hit the water, my voice went up an octave. I played gleefully and using the paddle fired streams of water at anyone I could see. Got a few of them, including Max.

Getting even wasn't easy. If you messed with the propman, then every time you picked up a suitcase it was full of bricks. Sometimes the propman had to be personally responsible for a prop he rented. If anything happened to it, he paid, not the studio. I finally saw my chance: an Italian motor scooter with sidecar. Joe was very nervous. I kept pestering him to let me ride it, so I could get used to it. "Well, okay," he said, "but only right around here where I can see you." Earlier, we had shot in the stage that was connected to ours by a huge sliding door. I motored the scooter sedately in small circles until he wasn't looking, then roared through the door into the other stage. The set we had used in there was a fully equipped restaurant kitchen. A buddy of mine pushed all the giant pots off the stove and threw all the silverware on the floor. The noise was stupendous. The scooter had to be totaled. The whole crew came running in, with Joe screaming, "Denver, you're paying, not me!" I was hidden behind a flat. There wasn't anything to see. "Where are you? What's going on? I'm losing my mind!" I started the scooter up, drove it over to him, and said, "Take it easy, Joe, the scooter's fine, so far," and went at full throttle back into the other stage with Joe running behind shouting, "Stop! Get off! Oh, you're going to be sorry, Denver!"

As a master propman, Joe had solutions for every problem. In one scene I had to carry six big bullfrogs in a cake box. They were supposed to leap out and scatter all over the place when I put the box down and opened it up. Only they lay there in a slimy mess. We did three takes. Since I was carrying them, I could tell each time that nothing was going to happen. The director yelled at Joe, "Come on, do something!" Joe said he would, but we could only do this one take, no more. I waited off camera and Joe waited for action before handing me the box. I could barely keep the lid down. When I opened it, the frogs took off like greased lightning. "How did you do it, Joe?" I asked. "Tabasco sauce," he answered.

In this instance, the propman was in charge of the frogs, but every other time I worked with an animal it came with a trainer. Except horses. They came with a wrangler. Go figure. The trainer, when asked if his particular animal could perform all the "acting" in the script, always said yes. After all, he had a couple of weeks to train it. There's nothing wrong with that; human actors do it all the time. Some of the animals I worked with in *Dobie* were a chimp, a lion, an elephant, a goat, a mynah bird, rabbits, a dog, a toucan, a petrified frog, and an eight-foot chicken. Working with the chimp gave me my first glimpse of what *wild* meant when applied to animals.

In the episode "Spaceville," Maynard was selected for a ground test by the army as the least likely to survive a missile launching. Maynard makes friends with a bright chimp and is accidentally launched with his fuzzy buddy in a real capsule, and together, they find peace and plenty on a remote island paradise. Pretty spooky, huh?

He was a cute little guy, about three or four years old, still young enough not to know how strong he was. At five or six they know. I don't work with those guys. The trainer, the chimp, and I were standing together waiting for the set to be lighted when the chimp grabbed my left hand and stuck it in his mouth up to midknuckle. He very gently, but firmly, bit down. When I tried to pull my fingers out, he bit down a little harder. We had a staring contest and I lost. I turned to the trainer and said, "Hey, I think we have a problem here." He took one look and turned a pasty white. Perspiration instantaneously sprang out on his forehead and upper lip. I'd never seen that happen before and I intuited I was in trouble. "Tell him to let go," I said. "I can't. He's testing you. If I do any-thing, he really will bite," he whispered. "Well, what am I supposed to do?" I whispered. Why we were whispering escaped me. Then he said, "You have to hit him in the forehead with the heel of your hand as hard as you can. Don't pull your punch and don't make a fist. His head is like concrete." Now, I knew why we were whispering. "Let me get this straight," I whispered. "I hit him as hard as I can with the heel of my hand right between the eyes and he will let go." "Yeah, and don't let him see it coming." I looked around the set and nobody was paying attention to us. They were all working, and what could they do to help? I glanced down at the chimp, who was dressed in an army uniform, a private, and thought, well, at least I can't be court-martialed for hitting an officer. I started talking to the trainer about the weather or some-thing; then I whirled and hit the chimp. He staggered back and let go. From that moment on, that chimp would do anything I asked him, and I had a bruised hand for a week. The trainer wished all actors would do the same. It made his job a piece of cake.

The next run-in with an animal was with the African lion. I arrived at the studio and saw the crew standing around an old pickup that was parked outside the stage. It had a handmade camper on it. I walked over and saw it was a cage with the lion in it. He was lying in the back and just staring out. The guys were saying things like, "He doesn't look so dangerous to me." "Just a big pussy cat." Then one of them went up to the bars and said, "Here, kitty, kitty." The lion let out a roar and charged the bars. Everybody scattered. "Glad you're working with him, not me," someone said. I was thinking, "Oh, boy, I have a scene with the lion, just the lion and me. Two pages of dialogue, a monologue. Oh, boy . . ."

The first "scene" I had with him was the two of us in a window looking out. Talk about bad breath! A diet of raw meat makes for a case of halitosis not to be believed. Also, I don't think he brushed twice a day. I only had a line or two and didn't need to rehearse. The trainer said, "Good." I wondered what that meant. This trainer had to be in his late sixties, frail looking, and smelled like the lion. He carried a six-foot broom handle. He did not inspire confidence. When we shot the scene, I peeked at the beast. His eyes resembled marbles. I don't think he knew I was there. He seemed really spaced.

After the scene, the trainer asked if he could take the lion back to his cage. He had parked the pickup in the stage. No argument. We all watched as he jumped on the back of the lion and rode him right up the ramp into the pickup. He used the broomstick to guide him. We all looked at each other but nobody could think of anything to say. A first.

Much too soon, my scene in the park with the lion arrived. All the lion had to do was walk in and lie down. The trainer proceeded to put four-foot chicken wire in front of the crew and cameras, encasing the park inside. Like a pen, with me inside with the lion. I had to ask the trainer what this was supposed to do. He said, "It's to keep the lion in the set. He might want to go back to his cage." Sure, a four-foot-high fence of chicken wire is going to stop a five-hundred-pound panicky beast. My confidence in the trainer, already at an all-time low, went further down.

The lion, meanwhile, was lying off camera, very calm. Nothing was bothering him. The director asked if I needed a rehearsal. Was he kidding? I had memorized this scene like no other in my life. I would say the words no matter what happened. The cameras rolled, the director called action, softly, the lion just lay there. He wouldn't get up. The trainer did everything he could think of to get him on his feet for his entrance. I was secretly hoping he'd never get up. Then I could do the scene by myself and they could film the lion by himself and cut him in with the appropriate reactions. But the special effects man had a suggestion. He had a pellet gun and he would shoot the lion in the ass and that would get him up. It was getting surreal. The effects man stood way back in the dark, where the lion couldn't see him, and shot him. The first shot perked the lion up. The second caused a low rumble and made him start looking for his tormentor. Unfortunately, that was the wrong direction for his entrance. The third shot really woke him up but still didn't get him to his feet. The fourth shot really pissed him off, and he zeroed in on the effects man as the source of his discomfort. Chicken wire or not, the effects man called it quits. Great. All he'd done was get the lion really angry. Thanks. The trainer finally got him to his feet, but now he wouldn't make his entrance, so he hit him in the balls with the broomstick. It got him moving, straight at me. He wasn't in a good frame of mind. As he got closer, I started my speech, realizing that this was going to be the only time we'd shoot this. I patted his head and he collapsed at my feet. I finished my lines. No take two.

When it was over, I thought to myself, "You did real good. You did it in one take and you were cool. Nobody would know how tense you were." When I saw the scene later, I thought I broke a record for how fast you can talk. If a pin had dropped, I would have gone a minimum of ten feet in the air, pieces of me flying in all directions. That whole day the lion acted like he was stoned. Well, he was. The trainer had doped him up so much, all he could do naturally was breathe. The director told the trainer to bring the lion in straight for the next day's shooting. He did.

The next day he was off drugs, wide-awake. Talk about being with it, this was a new lion. Eyes clear and very alert. We all thought we liked the old lion. There was a scene in the freezer of the Gillis grocery where the lion was supposed to lick some bones, causing Dobie and Maynard to think that he had eaten Mr. G. The trainer put cod-liver oil on the bones because it was a real favorite of the lion's. That explained the breath. We did the take and the director said get the lion out. Easier said than done. That lion was licking the bones like there was no tomorrow. The trainer finally used his infamous broomstick to sweep the bones away. With a deafening roar the lion broke the broomstick with his paw. We all took off. You could hear the staccato sound of the stage door opening and closing as people ran out. This wasn't easy to do because that door was big and weighed a ton. During the rest of the shooting, everybody kept a very wary eye on the lion. There were a lot more trips to the men's room than usual.

But enough of the animals, let's talk about the human actors.

WORKING WITH DWAYNE HICKMAN

I was very lucky to have Dwayne as the star of the series. He already had five years of experience, on the Bob Cummings show, *Love That Bob*. There weren't many actors in the fifties who could say that. He took the respon-

sibility seriously. He always knew his lines. I can't remember a time he forgot one in a scene with me. This gave me the freedom as an actor to concentrate on my character and have fun. This may not sound like much, but if you are working with an actor who messes up constantly, the scene never gets going and all you can think about is when it's going to happen. The stops and starts, pickups, and general confusion cause the scene to end up disjointed. Any flow is lost and so is the humor.

Dwayne also had to carry the show as Dobie. It meant that he was in almost every scene. He had monologues in front of the statue of The Thinker that would choke a horse. I'd be leaving to go home after shooting a show and see Dwayne sitting there getting ready to do them. They would save up lots of them from various shows so he would have to do them at one sitting. There is much to be said for being a supporting player. All I had to do was show up and do my scenes.

In the first year of the series Dwayne's hair was a pale blond. He had to get it bleached because its natural color was brown. When the second season began, he was back to brown. Dwayne asked whose idea it was in the first place for him to be blond. A dead silence. Whose idea it was still remains a mystery.

Dwayne drove a black, two-seater Mercedes that he had purchased when he was doing the Bob Cummings show. It was classic. I couldn't wait to get a new car and trade in my 1949 four-door Packard. At the end of the first year I got a white MGA roadster. "Going Hollywood" had its rewards.

Dwayne never acted like he was the star of the series. He shared the spotlight with everyone. I learned from him and used that when I later did *Gilligan*. I don't remember him losing his temper on the set. That I didn't learn. He was always warm and generous to the new kid, me. Thanks, Dwayne. Ya trained me good.

FRANK FAYLEN

In the first year of the show I met my first professional actors. People who actually made a living acting. I was anxious to join them. Frank Faylen was certainly a pro. He played Dobie's father, Mr. G., who owned a small grocery store and had a typical teenage son. His most frequent outburst was "I gotta kill that boy, I just gotta!" Max had created his character as a small-business man who by working long and hard was just barely making it. Yet in the same small town was the unbelievably rich Osborne family. This was in the late 1950s, so nobody questioned how realistic this all was.

Frank had started out as a hoofer back in vaudeville and then got small parts in the movies. You see him every year as the cabdriver in *It's a Wonderful Life*. He was as generous as Dwayne was to the new kid on the set. Frank loved to

yne did his best to go beatnik, but
d never pass. It's in the blood, man.

do physical comedy, but we all learned to get the hell out of the way when he was careening around. The one time that stands out was when Frank was to do a tumbling routine. He was dressed in a short toga, and as he did his somersault, the whole crew burst out laughing. The director shouted cut and asked, "What's wrong with you guys? That wasn't funny. Come on, give the old guy a break. That was a great somersault, Frank! Okay, let's try it again." Nobody said a word. Frank looked a little hurt, but he was a trouper. As he did his somersault in the second take, the director's eyes bulged out and he screamed, "Cut! Frank! Frank! What are you doing? You don't have any underwear on!" As Frank did his somersault, the skirt of the toga flipped up, exposing everything. To this day, I'm not sure whether Frank did it on purpose or not.

Frank and I used to go to a bowling alley during the lunch break with some of the crew. There was no commissary on the lot. We shot at what was called Fox Western, a little studio left over from the early days. It wasn't in the greatest neighborhood. In fact, prostitutes worked the alley only a couple of blocks away. There were basically three places to eat: the bowling alley, a bar/restaurant where the food was secondary to the booze, and a place run by little old ladies, The League of something or other, where the food leaned toward tea sandwiches and very bland entrées. We alternated between the three. I guess the bar got most of the business.

Frank was competitive. He threw the bowling ball straight at the pins as hard as he could. It was airborne for the first ten feet. We played on teams—the actors against the crew. It wasn't unusual for Frank's ball to hit the headpin causing it to fly into the next alley and either cause a strike or spare for the competition. Our opponents loved Frank. One time, Frank and I weren't in the shot after lunch, so we got to stay an extra half hour. I rolled a scratch 222. This, for me, was the same as a perfect game. We rushed back to the studio and told the crew. "Oh, yeah. Sure," they said. "Frank was there!" I said. They started laughing and said, "Frank? Come on. You actors stick together and Frank would back you up no matter what you said."

Frank was hurt. They didn't believe him. I really didn't care, but he was upset. I told him to forget it. It didn't matter. It did to him. All afternoon he sulked around and gave the crew bad looks. They loved it and teased him more. Even the next day at the bowling alley he was still pissed off. He was throwing his ball so hard, it was dangerous to be near him. In the second game my ball took on a life of its own. I rolled 222. This was the second time I'd done it and was the last. I never again in my life scored that high. Frank was in seventh heaven. He marched around shouting, "I told you! You didn't believe me! Now what do you have to say?" He gave me a hug and went on and on.

Preceding page: Mr. G. (Frank Faylen), Dobie, and me in an arresting scene.

38

The crew didn't hear the last of it for months. It wasn't long after that the lunch hours were spent at the bar/restaurant.

Frank also had a problem with his permanent dressing room. This was located at the back of the lot, a long way from the stage. Most of us didn't use them because of that. Not Frank. Having a permanent dressing room meant a step up in the actor's world. He used it. One day he came to me and said that something was going on in his dressing room. Once a week, when he came in the morning, he would find towels strewn about, with makeup on them. Somebody was using *his* dressing room!

He checked out all the shows that were shooting on the lot and found no suspects. He was losing it. Months went by, but there didn't seem to be a pattern. Sometimes it was a Tuesday, then a Wednesday. Sometimes once a week or once every two weeks. He was losing it. He was determined to catch the trespasser. He started staking out his dressing room. I'd see him the morning after one of his stakeouts. His eyes were red from no sleep and his temper was short. He'd stay up all night on a Tuesday, and of course, it was Wednesday it got used. Then, abruptly, I heard no more. Had he caught the culprit? It wasn't like Frank to be so silent. I asked him what had happened. He mumbled something about everything being okay. I said, "What do you mean okay? What happened?"

It seemed he was staked out in his car, watching his dressing room, at two-thirty A.M. when it happened. A car drove up and two people got out and went into his dressing room. Frank leaped out of his car and flung open the door and screamed, "I got you! I finally got you!" What he had gotten was a sergeant from the LAPD with a hooker. A brief discussion ensued. The end result was the dressing room could be used whenever. Frank sighed, "At least I don't have to worry about parking tickets anymore."

Frank couldn't understand why Max wouldn't write a script that used his talent as a dancer. He was always telling me it was stupid not to use him. Those days of dancing onstage on the vaudeville circuit were not to be wasted. How many series had an actor who could do the old soft shoe? I said I didn't know but probably not many and why tell me. Tell Max. Near the end of the first year he got his wish. A script came out with Frank saving the day with the unused talent. You would have thought he was going to do a command performance for the queen the way he rehearsed. The day of shooting arrived and he was in a tizzy. Max had teased him for weeks. "I think we'd better hire a choreographer for this sequence," he said. Frank went ballistic. Then Max would say things like, "Script looks long. May have to cut the end, or at least trim it down. Hey, Frank, how long is your routine?" Until we shot the scene, he never knew if it was going to be in the show. We finally did it. Frank was great. He hoofed it all over the place. He was the happiest I'd ever seen him and from then on the easiest actor to work with. Max said, "If I'd known this was going to happen, he would have danced in the second episode!"

FLORIDA FRIEBUS

Florida Friebus played Frank's wife, Winifred Gillis. She was a stage actress with a wealth of experience. (She was a longtime colleague of Eva Le Gallienne.) I think this is why she ended up with all the exposition. That's an acting term. It means the plot advanced when she spoke her lines. There is no duller role for an actor. You get the feeling the scenery is more interesting. She never had a joke, always played straight, and she did it perfectly. It finally got to her in the third year. She asked for a comedy scene so she could do some of the jokes. Since she never complained about anything, the writers complied. Unfortunately, the scene wasn't funny and the jokes stank. She said she thought it would be better if she stayed with what she'd been doing. She was a great lady, and really, the only time she complained was when we spent the whole day shooting in the grocery store set. Then, with a clear voice and projection, so the last row in the balcony could hear her, she would say, "Mother's melting!" She was justified.

Dwayne, Frank, Florida, and I made up the regular cast. I couldn't have asked for better actors to help me learn my craft. Always supportive. They showed me how a professional actor should behave. After all, I was one now. I was being paid the enormous sum of $250 an episode. It may not sound like much, but I was earning a living doing what I loved.

The other actors who worked on the show were semiregulars. In the first year there were Tuesday Weld, Warren Beatty, Sheila James, William Schallert, Steve Franken, and Doris Packer. They were all excellent to work with and learn from.

TUESDAY WELD

Tuesday was something else. I believe she was fifteen and a half years old when she started on the show in 1959. It was hard to tell. She had already appeared in the film version of Max's *Rally 'Round the Flag, Boys!* She showed up for work always prepared and was polite to me. I knew I wasn't in the same league as her. Not even the same ballpark. The press was all over her. I'd never seen this brand of frenzy before. She had done some movies that had been successful, and she was being touted as an up-and-coming young star. National media, local media, Cleveland media, everybody wanted interviews, pictures. She was hot. She was also a good actress. I had watched the circus from a ringside seat on the set. Between takes she was besieged. At the end of the first year she decided to call the whole thing off. No more press. Not even the biggies. Can't say that I blame her. She also said that she wouldn't do any more TV. When she came back in the third year, there was absolutely no press. In fact, in the time that had passed I had seen nothing about her. The publicity man for the studio said that when she cut off the press, at first they didn't believe it. Then for the first time in his memory, they banded together and vowed they would never print her name again. I was amazed. The competition was fierce in the media; it was unheard of for all of them to stay resolute. I guess they wanted to show their power. Her career came to a near stop, and I think even today there's some of that spite left. It was too bad because Tuesday was well on the way to becoming a big star.

I, on the other hand, was just starting out, and doing press was exciting. I said yes to anything. Not that there was that much. Dwayne was the star and handled the brunt of it. It wasn't until *Gilligan* that I understood Tuesday's dilemma.

WARREN BEATTY

Warren Beatty's agent obviously goofed when he got him the part of the rich kid, Milton Armitage. He was great in the part, but we all sensed that he was not long for episodic TV. Someone whispered to me that Shirley MacLaine was his sister. I said, who's she? I was really a novice in show biz. One incident with Mr. Beatty that stands out was when someone locked him in a dressing room onstage. It was one those flimsy kinds with canvas walls. He shouted a few times to be let out and then became silent. It wasn't until the middle of the next take that we heard from him. He was singing opera at the top of his lungs. The director stopped the scene and asked what the hell was going on. Beatty was quickly let out. I thought it was pretty cool the way he reacted. He didn't stay with the series very long. I think it was only for five or six episodes. Less than a year later he was in the film *Splendor in the Grass* and he was on his way. Nobody on the *Dobie* set was too surprised.

SHEILA JAMES AND THE REST OF THE GANG

Sheila played Zelda Gilroy, a girl who was determined to have Dobie. Nothing would stop her. Sheila was excellent in the part. She had been a child actress in an earlier series and had vast television experience. I was surrounded by pros. They were everywhere. She always knew her lines, and sometimes it seemed she knew everyone else's. If I forgot mine, she would give it to me.

One day, I saw her in the corner of the set, going over the next week's script. It looked suspiciously like she was memorizing each page. Her finger would run down the page and then she would nod slightly. As a joke I went over to her and said, "What are you doing—memorizing the whole thing?" Startled, she looked up and said, "Please don't tell anyone!" She had a semi-photographic memory. When I had scenes with her, I couldn't have felt more secure. She was always fun to work with and was with the series all four years. After the series ended she went to law school and graduated first in her class. She's a lawyer now in L.A.

Steve Franken took over the part of the rich kid, Chatsworth Osborne, Jr., after Warren Beatty left and ran with it. He was great as the spoiled kid. Steve is a good actor and it was a pleasure to watch him work. Chatsworth's mother was played by Doris Packer. She was a tried-and-true character actress. I used to have lunch with her and listen to her tips on acting. I learned a lot. In fact, I was surrounded by actors who had experience and talent. There was Bill Schallert as the teacher. He would later star as Patty Duke's TV father as well as in dozens of other roles. Some of the other actors who came through were Bill Bixby, Mel Blanc (who was worn to a frazzle doing his voices), Francis X. Bushman (from the silent days), Ryan O'Neal, Ron Howard (as a little guy), Rose Marie, Jo Anne Worley, Sally Kellerman, and Burt Metcalfe. Who? Burt was a man who started his acting career when he was in his seventies. He worked all the time. It made me feel that maybe I'd chosen the right line of work.

LEARNING TO BE A TV STAR

This was also the time I started signing autographs. I don't think anyone really understands this behavior. I've been signing for thirty-three years and it still fascinates me. If I start to get a big head, I remember what happened to me when I was signing pictures at Universal. For three weekends was in the booth at the entrance to the tour. The people couldn't miss me. I signed hundreds of pictures. Fans came up from all over the world. A Greek family was convinced I spoke Greek because the show was dubbed in their language.

Zelda Gilroy was the queen of unrequited love, though Dobie seldom noticed.

42

Try explaining dubbing to someone who doesn't speak English. I told them I didn't speak Greek. They all laughed, knowing better, got their pictures, and left.

By the Sunday of the third weekend I was swollen with ego. During a break, I noticed a man dressed as a bus driver staring at me in disgust. He was giving me dirty looks every time I looked at him. I called him over and asked, haughtily, "What's your problem?" He said, "I'll tell you what my problem is. It's all those goddamn pictures you're signing! I drive one of those big tour buses, bring all those nuts here, and take them back! I just want to go home when I'm done, but, oh, no, I've got to spend an extra fifteen or twenty minutes picking up those pictures. They're all over the bus. Stuck in the seats, under the seats, everywhere!" You could hear the air escaping from my head. It straightened me right out. A little humble pie is good for the system.

Doing Maynard also introduced me to the world of personal appearances. The one that stands out happened at Lake Ponchartrain, just outside New Orleans. Forty thousand people came to watch me pick a mate for Maynard. On the stage were seven girls dressed as beatniks. I was supposed to hold my hand over each contestant's head and judge by the applause who was the winner. The roar sounded the same every time. I was starting to panic. The mob was closing in on the stage. I picked a girl and ran. Four big troopers were waiting backstage. They ordered me to hold on to the belts of the ones in front and in back of me. We plowed our way to a waiting jeep and took off down the beach. Lucky for me, the lights were turned off and a fireworks show started.

In the middle 1970s I shot a pilot that updated *Dobie Gillis*. The stage manager said there were some Maynard fans in the audience and would I go out to say hello to them. The show had been off the air for more than ten years and I thought he was putting me on. Not so. There were about twenty beatniks sitting out there. Beards, long hair, and shades. Stoned out of their gourds. I said, "Hi," and they mumbled something. I made a fast exit. Makes you wonder about the effect of television.

I did personal appearances all four years of *Dobie* when I found that you could get money for them. In fact, after a while I made more from them than I was making playing Maynard. My salary went up a hundred dollars more an episode. By the start of the fourth year, I realized that I wasn't being paid what other actors earned for the same job. I heard for the first time that magic word *renegotiate*. My agent told the studio that if I didn't get a raise, I wouldn't show up. Max said, "Fine, we'll get another actor." My agent said, "He's bluffing." I said, "Max doesn't know that word." I went to work. They did agree to pay me a bonus if I was "heavy" in an episode. The only trouble with that was, they

decided what "heavy" meant. I think I collected the bonus three times out of thirty-five.

All in all, the four years of *Dobie Gillis* taught me how lucky I was. Being in the right place at the right time was the secret. There are thousands of good actors out of work because the stars haven't crossed at the right time yet. Of course, when the series ended, I thought I'd never work again. We had wrapped in February of '63 and nothing much happened, work-wise, for months. That summer Megan, my daughter, was born, and when I came home from the hospital, there was a residual check in the mailbox. "Great," I thought. "I can pay the hospital." The check was for thirty cents. I kept putting it in the envelope and taking it out again, thinking the decimal point would change. Thirty cents had to be a mistake. It wasn't. In the fall of that year I met with the writer Sherwood Schwartz about a proposed pilot. Financially, I was broke. I thought, "Just in time. I'll get a check for the pilot and that will carry me through Christmas. Who cares if it goes to series." Who knew?

Dobie (Dwayne Hickman) and Zelda (Sheila James) and an unidentified Chinese cook. Dig Dobie's snow white hair! It was dyed blond for the first season.

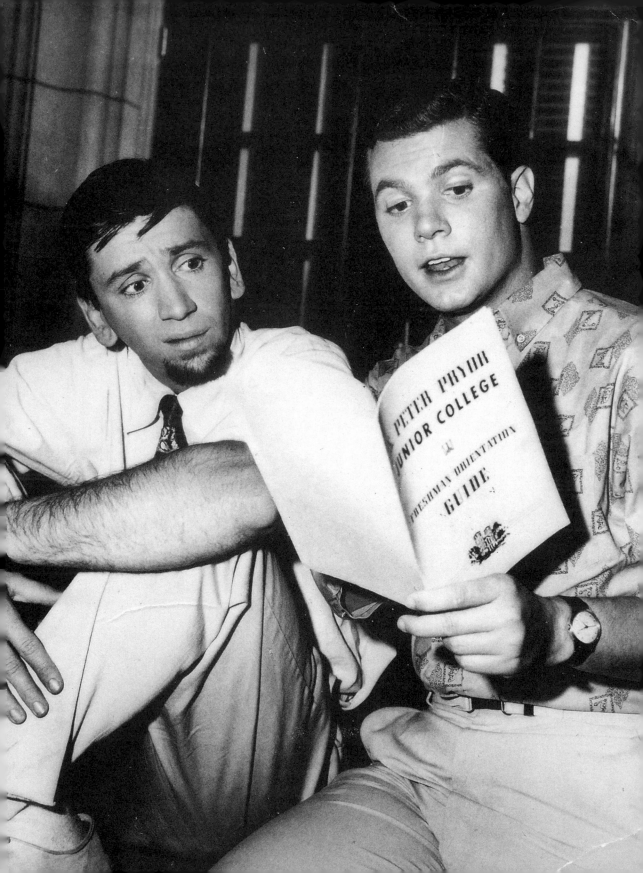

MY FAVORITE *DOBIE GILLIS* EPISODES

"GREATER LOVE HATH NO MAN"

Maynard falls for Dobie's girl. This didn't happen very often—in fact, hardly ever. Dobie has to choose between love and friendship. In a dream sequence, Dobie plays Cyrano de Bergerac for Maynard. The girl finds out the truth and dumps them both. Nothing new for Dobie.

Dream sequences allowed the show to expand and the story to go wild with full costume, wigs, and makeup. Dwayne looked great as Cyrano. I realized that we weren't going to be stuck only doing scenes in the grocery store or the high school. When you get to play a different character, the acting becomes fun to do.

"MAYNARD'S FAREWELL TO THE TROOPS"

Maynard feels rejected and joins the army. Heavy acting involved in this one. His cousin comes to live with his parents and takes his place.

I was written out of the show! I couldn't believe that this was to be my last show of the series. The next week I had to report for induction in the army. It was very depressing. My big show biz break was over before it even got started. I said good-bye to everyone on the last day of shooting. When the army didn't want me, I went back to the set and no one believed it. Max finally understood and said, "Go home. Just go home. We'll call you." Three days later he did and I was back on the series. Yahoo!

"SOUP AND FISH"

A socialite girl and her wealthy beatnik girlfriend invite Dobie and Maynard to a

would never have gotten through my first audition
without Dwayne. Thanks, buddy.

swank party. They convince the rich kid Chatsworth to share his tux because they don't have one. Each one takes turns wearing it. The hit of the party is Maynard. The beatnik girl falls for him.

In this episode I finally met another actor who had to play a beatnik. She asked me for tips on how to play the part. I said, "Hey, chick! Just let it flow, you know? Be hip and talk about poetry and jazz. Remember you're anti just about everything. You're a protest cat. Be cool." She laughed and said, "Okay, man. I dig where you're coming from. I'll be the hippest chick you've ever seen!" When we did our scenes together, everybody shook their heads in confusion. Were there really people like this out in the real world?

It was during the scene when we were sharing the tux that I learned the first rule of wardrobe comedy. When being filmed in your underwear, it has to be funny underwear. Boxer shorts, of course. Mine had big red hearts all over them.

"BABY SHOES"

Dobie and Maynard join the army. Mr. G. has Dobie's baby shoes bronzed as a cherished memory. Maynard has his sneakers bronzed to take with him into the army. It seems I couldn't stay out of the army!

I had those bronzed sneakers in my possession for years, but lost them in my wanderings. If you know where they are, please tell me. They have a special place in my heart.

"THE BIG QUESTION"

Dobie and Maynard have to write an essay titled "Whither Are We Drifting?" to graduate from high school. It makes them realize that they don't know what they're going to do after school ends, and they become fearful.

This script had a serious side to it. It presented a problem all high school kids have to face. Sometimes Max liked to do a script that slipped in a serious message. He was always surprising us.

"DOBIE PLAYS CUPID"

Dobie tries to bolster Maynard's confidence with girls. Good luck. He finds out that Maynard isn't afraid of girls; he just wants to pursue his own way of life.

I got to explain Maynard's philosophy of life in this episode. He was a true free spirit. He never wanted to be tied down to anything. When I read the script, there was a one-word line, "Work!" and in parenthesis after it the words *He reacts*. I spent hours saying the word until one reading sounded right. Little did I know how many more times I'd have to say, "Work!" and react with that frantic shirk.

Maynard's reaction to that four-letter word started innocently enough, but by the end of the show it was his trademark. Recently, I was sitting on a plane in the window seat when a businessman sat down next to me. He pulled down the tray, opened his briefcase, and started to work (work!). As the passengers filed past, every tenth one yelled "Work!" at me. The businessman thought they were shouting at him. He got more and more flustered, until he just shut the briefcase and turned to me and said, "Why are they shouting at me? I always do my work on the plane!" I took off my shades and said they were talking to me. He did a double take and said, "Oh, it's you. Thank God. I thought I was losing my mind!"

It's hard to live down being Maynard G. Krebs.

"Baby Talk"

Maynard finds a baby abandoned in the park and decides to keep it. Mrs. Osborne won't let him. Good thinking. They find the parents and the baby is reunited with them.

This was the first time I had worked with a baby. There is an old show business rule that says you should never work with kids or animals. I've spent my career breaking that rule. In one scene the little tyke babbled all through my lines. I just kept going and they used it. In another, the baby sneezed and I said, "God bless you," and kept going. Jo Anne Worley played the baby's mom. This was before her opera-aria days on Laugh-In.

"The Battle of Maynard's Beard"

The army orders Maynard to shave his goatee. He refuses, giving examples of all the bearded generals through history. A court-martial is held. The head judge is an officer with a beard. Guess what? Maynard wins.

I was afraid that I was going to have to shave my goatee off and wear a fake one. They are the worst. The glue itches and you can't move your lower lip, so you end up talking like you have a mouthful of marbles. Plus, I used to say my lines at a speed that approached the sound barrier. After a scene was shot, the director would call out to the soundman, "Was that understandable?" The soundman would play back the scene through his earpiece and shout back, "Yeah, all the key words were there!"

"I Didn't Raise My Boy to Be a Soldier, Sailor, or Marine"

Maynard misses the bus on his first day in the army. Chatsworth gets roped in to pretend to be Maynard until he shows up. When he does, Chatsworth has done so well, Maynard is eligible for Officer Candidate School. He turns it down because he thinks Dobie needs him more.

Steve Franken was great in this episode. As Chatsworth, he was embarrassed to have to pretend to be Maynard. What was more embarrassing for me was when Dwayne, I, and four extras were doing army calisthenics, including jumping jacks, and I farted. The director yelled cut and said, "All right, which one of you did that?" I looked around at the other guys and they looked around at each other, and nobody said anything. I breathed a sigh of relief. I had avoided the teasing the crew would have heaped on me.

Take two. Right in the middle of the jumping jacks I let another one go. This time the extras, the crew, and everyone within earshot pointed at me. No escape. I suffered in silence while everybody got their shots in. Ah, the life of a professional actor.

"MAYNARD G. KREBS, BOY MILLIONAIRE"

Maynard finds a purse, and when it goes unclaimed, he gets the money that was in it. Some con men try to get the money from Maynard.

I had a great time doing this episode because the con artists were played by Jack Albertson, Joey Faye, and Milton Frome, whose careers stretched back to the days of vaudeville. You may remember Albertson as "the man" in *Chico and the Man*. They told great stories and jokes. They treated me as their equal and I felt like I was really in show business. The Hollywood Square Dancers were on the show, too. Kind of an oxymoron, eh?

"SPACEVILLE"

As discussed earlier, in this episode Maynard is launched into space with a chimp and lands on a desert island.

I had never seen a chimp lose his temper before. The trainer wanted him to do something and offered him a hard candy, then when he didn't obey, took it back. This went on five or six times, then

all hell broke loose. The chimp went into a full-blown temper tantrum: teeth bared, screaming, and stomping off the set. Scary. The trainer said for everyone not to move. This was getting to be the usual refrain from the trainers with all the animals I worked with. You could hear him wandering around the stage as we waited. Dwayne was coming out of his dressing room as the chimp went by, and he took three quick steps back and slammed the door. I told the trainer please not to use this method of enticement anymore. I was the one who had to work with him. This was the same chimp that took a liking to my fingers.

"WHAT'S MY LION"

A valuable sacred lion, a gift of a powerful Eastern potentate to the local zoo, escapes and attaches himself to Maynard. Being a free-spirited beatnik, he wants the lion returned to the jungle. It turns out the potentate is also a jazz fan, so he digs Maynard's message and the lion goes free.

I learned my first lesson when working with wild animals. Always remember the word *wild* means exactly that. It does not mean tame or friendly. Unpredictability is the norm. A lion is not a "big pussycat." Do not try to make friends. Stay away at all times; you don't want the animal to remember you. Be prepared at all times to run for your life.

"I WAS A BOY SORORITY GIRL"

Dobie falls for a snobbish society girl. Since he never has any money, he takes a job as a waiter at a sorority party. Maynard tags along. The girl shows up at the party and Dobie and Maynard put on dresses to hide from her. I hid my goatee with a scarf. Even Mr. G. gets into the act, dressing up as Dobie's mother. When the truth comes out, Mr. G. is barred from the campus, Dobie is put on probation, and Maynard can't get rid of a delivery boy, who refuses to believe he isn't a girl.

There must be an unwritten rule that states all series must have an episode where the cast has to dress up as the opposite sex. I don't mean women playing men. It's always the other way around. Talk about discrimination. And I really make an ugly girl. It doesn't make any difference how hard the makeup man tries, the results are always the same.

"SWEET SUCCESS OF SMELL"

Maynard develops an uncanny sense of smell and can track down lost objects. He and Dobie open the Private Nose Agency to track down anything that has been lost.

Danielle De Metz) may look like a beatnik
, but she's really just French. This show,
ez-vous English," is one of the few in which
to steal the girl from Dobie.

This episode was shot in the third year and I could sense that my character was starting to lean toward the type of comedy that I really liked to play. Fantasy ridiculous. Maynard was beginning to break out of the realm of reality, not that he was ever too tied down in the first place. This series was getting to be fun.

"THE TRUTH SESSION"

Maynard is afraid of flunking a class, so he concocts an excuse that is so outrageous and obvious a lie, it gets accepted. Even when he admits it was a lie, he gets a passing grade for telling the truth. Convinced that telling the truth is the way to go, he gives it out in great chunks to everyone he meets. Nobody wants to hear it and fights break out all over the town. Eventually, everyone is humbled and Maynard says that if they all play their cards right from now on, he will never try to "help" them again by telling the truth about them.

I think every one wishes that, one time, they could do what Maynard did. It was great fun to be able to do it on the series. Though it was secondhand, I still enjoyed it. The best was catching Mr. G. in all the lies he was capable of. Maynard left him yelling and sputtering all over the store. It was fortunate that Maynard was such an innocent, otherwise he would have got punched out. Many of the *Dobie* scripts had real good messages in them. It wasn't all fun and games.

"TOO MANY KOOKS SPOIL THE BROTH"

Dobie is in love with Cecily, whose father is the kitchenware king of America. He signs up for an executive training course taught by the father. Virgil, Dobie's cousin, shows up and takes the class, too. He wants to marry Cecily and be rich. Dobie does a demonstration of a Quick Cooker to impress Cecily. Maynard helps and everything blows up. Virgil gets the girl and leaves town.

The director for this episode was our film editor. It was his first time out as a director. The scene where the large pots blew up worried him. He wanted the effect to work perfectly, so he told the crew he wanted it done by the "numbers." They all stared at him like he'd lost his mind. There were only three steps to the gag. One, a long trough of black powder went off behind the pots. Two, the lids of the pots went up in the air. They were attached by monofilament to fishing poles that were held by men up high on the catwalk over the set. They'd just pull them up. Three, more men up high would throw down vegetables after the lids were "blown" off. Pretty simple. All it required was the word *action*. But noooo! By the numbers. Our director rehearsed the scene over and over. ONE. Explosion! TWO. Lids!! THREE. Vegetables!!! By now, a considerable crowd had gathered in disbelief. The cameras finally rolled and the director took a deep breath and shouted, "*Two!* No. *One!* I mean, *Three.* No. No. *Two! One! Three! One! Two!* Oh, God!" The crew did it by the numbers. The lids went up, the explosion went off, the vegetables came down, the lids came down and went back up, more vegetables came down, chaos reigned supreme. Moral: Let the crew do its job.

"THE LITTLE CHIMP THAT COULDN'T"

Maynard rescues a little chimp from medical research, but he must teach him certain tricks in order to save him. He fails to do this, so he paints some pictures, saying the chimp did them. Since they're extremely crude and primitive, he's believed. The dean of the college, however, wants to see the chimp do the paintings. As he watches, the little guy paints perfect replicas of *Blue Boy*, *Mona Lisa*, and other masterpieces.

The chimp in this show was a baby and real cute. Not dangerous at all. The only problem was he wanted to eat the paint. Because he was so much fun to work with, I decided to get a monkey for myself. Not taking any chances, I bought a pygmy marmoset. She was about four inches in height and ate a grape a day. Real tiny. I'd bought her in New York City and had her in the overhead compartment in a shoe box on the flight back to L.A. The man sitting next to me put a box up there, too. I waited awhile and then stood up to check that my box was still okay. He waited awhile, got up, and rearranged the boxes again. I got up. He got up. I finally said, "Listen, I have a tiny monkey in my box. I want to make sure she's getting air." He said, "I've got three live Maine lobsters in my box, and I've got the same problem." We arranged the boxes so everybody could breathe. Ever since I've always wondered just what could be in the overhead.

"I WAS A SPY FOR THE F.O.B."

The Gillises and Maynard take a trip to Washington, D.C. Two spies for a foreign government mistake Maynard for a renowned scientist and try to kidnap him. The FBI shows up and captures them.

This was one of the few shows where we shot the whole thing on different sets. It was a relief to get out of the grocery store and the classroom. Barbara Bain played one of the spies. Later, she showed up in *The Harlem Globetrotters on Gilligan's Island* along with her husband and *Mission: Impossible* costar Martin Landau. She basically played the same part. Accent and all. We laughed at how things come around. Instead of trying to seduce me, she went after the Professor. It was good thing Tina Louise refused to do that movie. She could have taken lessons from Barbara on seduction.

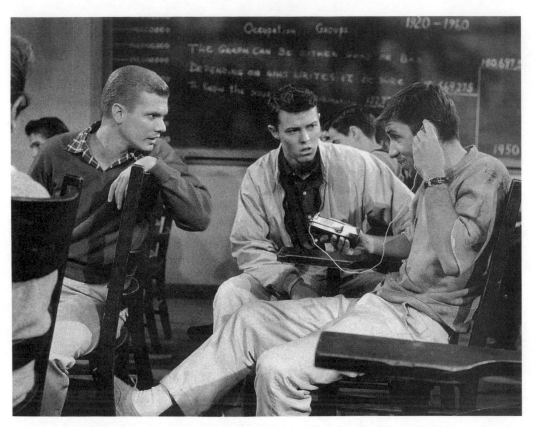

Maynard even brought his bee-bop to class.

"DR. JEKYLL AND MR. GILLIS"

Maynard sneaks into the chemistry lab and drinks a potion to make him smart, so he can pass his exams. He does, but the dean is suspicious. Wouldn't you be? Panicked, Maynard drinks too much and turns into Mr. Hyde. He creeps around town scaring everybody. An antidote is used on him and he turns into a professor, Mr. G., and a beautiful girl. Eventually, he becomes himself again.

As Mr. Hyde I had to have a full beard and hair all over my arms and the backs of my hands. The director wanted to see the transformation as Maynard changed into Mr. Hyde. This meant lying absolutely still for an hour on the floor with my head wedged in a corner. Lon Chaney, Jr., when he became the Wolfman, always found a crook of a tree to wedge his head in. The camera would roll a few feet of film and stop. The makeup man would add some more hair and the camera rolled again. This went on until I was fully made up. Plugs in my nostrils and hair everywhere. Basically, it was time-lapse photography.

My favorite scene was when Maynard, as Mr. Hyde, picked up the Gillis grocery store and shook it, with Mr. G. inside.

During the lunch break, I walked to the restaurant at the corner of Sunset and Western, in full makeup, with my three-year-old son, Patrick, in my arms. Cars were slamming on their brakes as people stared.

"CALL OF THE LIKE WILD"

Maynard accidently uses some oil from the biology class on his hair. He becomes irresistible to women. Mr. G. decides he will make him the new Valentino. He gets Maynard and a famous Italian movie actress together and she falls hard for him and wants him to be her leading man in her next movie. The picture is completed but flops when the audience can't smell Maynard.

Frank, as Maynard's agent, was far-out. He really got into it. He based the characterization on an old booker he knew in the 1930s. He even chomped a cigar.

It was during this episode or around this time that a rumor swept the country that I had been killed. Apparently a radio had fallen into my bathtub and electrocuted me. Wow! The first I heard of it was when the wire services started calling my house, after the thing started. Talk about shutting the barn door after the horse runs out. At first, I thought it was one of my friends putting me on, but after ten or more calls in thirty minutes, I believed that I was dead. It was bizarre. I was just getting used to people screaming when they saw me when the rumor slowly died out. It lasted about a year. Needless to say, since that time, I've never had a radio in my bathroom.

"THE BEAST WITH TWENTY FINGERS"

Maynard and Mr. G. become inseparable when their index fingers are locked together by a double-finger gripper. Mr. G. wants to go to a grocers' convention, but not if he has to drag Maynard along. Mrs. G. suggests that Maynard lose his beard and go as his wife. Maynard goes as the woman married to Herbert T. It's a mess.

I don't know why I had to dress up as a female all the time. Nobody else in the cast seemed to have to. I really was an ugly woman—maybe that was the reason. The little doodad that held Frank's finger and mine together was a tube, made of woven raffia. You pushed in and it opened up. When you pulled it apart, it tightened on your finger. I think every kid has had one and knows how it works. That we couldn't get loose was a weak premise. Still, being dragged around by Frank had some good moments. The only trouble that occurred was when our fingers swelled up and we really couldn't get the damn thing off. The propman had to cut it in half, with a great many jokes.

"EAT, DRINK, AND BE MERRY, FOR TOMORROW, KERBOOM"

The college is going to put a new time capsule on the campus. The history teacher wants ideas as to what the capsule should contain. Maynard is not interested. He believes the world is going to be blown up by the powers that be. He goes around predicting doom for all. That is, until the old time capsule is dug up and a 1914 newspaper headline predicts war and the end of the world. Obviously, everybody's time seems the worst in history.

We shot this episode not too long after the Cuban missile crisis. It was funny, but at the same time scary. Everyone was building or thinking about building bomb shelters in their backyards. Not me. The whole idea that you would survive an atomic blast seemed ludicrous. Still, there was always talk on the stage about what if? Looking back now, it's hard to believe that time. Anyway, Maynard's philosophy seemed to be the only answer.

"A FUNNY THING HAPPENED TO ME ON THE WAY TO A FUNNY THING"

A man is going to commit suicide by jumping off the ledge of a building. Maynard goes out to him and offers to jump with him. Shaken, the man reconsiders and climbs back in. Maynard falls from the ledge into a fireman's net and is taken to the psycho ward. He's tested and is found to be nuttier than a fruitcake. When the psychiatrists find out why he was really out on the ledge, they release him. He's a hero. Later, Dobie and Maynard see the same man about to jump off a cliff. Dobie insists on being the hero, but it backfires when the man jumps, taking Dobie with him.

This kind of plot became common during the fourth year of the series. The far-out kind. The main reason I had more to do on the series was that Dwayne got sick and needed time off. I ended up as the main character, carrying the story. This to me was great fun. I could make believe I was the star for a week. Also, the scripts, as you've probably noticed, had the best titles.

"WILL THE REAL SANTA CLAUS PLEASE COME DOWN THE CHIMNEY"

Maynard comes to live with the Gillises during the holidays, and they are shocked to find out he still believes in Santa. They're determined to bring him to his senses. Mr. G. is going to play Santa and then reveal himself to Maynard, but he gets stuck in the chimney. After building a new fireplace so he can shock Maynard, the whole plot collapses. On Christmas Eve, Maynard insists he wants nothing for himself and begs Santa to bring gifts to the Gillises. Shamed, Mr. G. rushes out to buy presents for everyone.

Every season we did a Christmas episode. It always revolved around Maynard and his childlike outlook on life. One year he was the ghost of Christmas past and haunted Dobie. I thought having an episode like this on shows during the holiday season made sense. Unfortunately, as the years went by, they died out. The reasoning was that during syndication, the Christmas episode could be aired at any time. Really, who cares?

"WHAT'S A LITTLE MURDER BETWEEN FRIENDS"

Dobie proposes to Thalia for the umpteenth time. She wants to know what he's worth. Maynard thinks she's a greedy, money-crazy chick. Dobie's only asset is his $10,000 GI life-insurance policy. He makes Thalia the beneficiary. Weird things start to happen to him and he thinks everybody is out to kill him. It turns out to be just a surprise party in his honor.

In 1988, we shot a TV reunion movie called *Bring Me the Head of Dobie Gillis*. It wasn't until I was doing research for this book that I realized that Max had taken the plot from this episode. He never stopped recycling scripts. The only problem was that Tuesday couldn't do it and it was aired against a killer miniseries. I don't think too many viewers saw it, but keep looking; it's bound to show up again.

HERE ON GILLIGAN'S ISLE

WORKING WITH SHERWOOD SCHWARTZ

As I mentioned, I met with Sherwood Schwartz in the fall of 1963 to discuss a new series. He explained the premise of the show as a microcosm of society with broad comedy. Seven people stranded on an island. I was hooked. One of my favorite books as a kid had been *Robinson Crusoe*. I later found out it was one of Sherwood's as well. I asked him if I could do physical comedy. I really wanted to do all those old slapstick sight gags. For some reason they attracted me—maybe because they had to be timed perfectly. They never seemed to go out of style. The ones from the silent days still made people laugh. Sherwood said that *Gilligan* was perfect for that kind of comedy.

I asked him to tell me some of the plots. He said that besides the usual ones of trying to survive on a deserted island, there would be guest stars. Guest stars? I could understand how they could get on the island, but when they left, wouldn't they tell where the island was located? We'd get rescued and that was the end of the series. He told me of his idea of a surfer who rode a giant tidal wave to the island, then rode a reverse tidal wave back to Hawaii. He hits his head on some rocks and can't remember where the island was. In fact, he can't remember much of anything. He told me a few more, and when I could get up off the floor, I said I really wanted to do this series. I loved silly comedy.

I asked him who was going to play the other parts. He said that he was going to interview and test for the other characters. I thought, that's six roles to fill, and started to admire Sherwood. He not only had a great sense of humor but was dedicated, too. As I talked to him, I realized he was very intelligent. Later, I found out he had two degrees. He had been heading for medical school when he took a job writing jokes for Bob Hope. I guess he got hooked, too. Recently he had been head writer for Red Skelton. This was to be his first go at a series.

I can honestly say that without Sherwood there would be no *Gilligan's Island*. What he went through to get the pilot sold is a lesson in perseverance, a quality he has in overabundance. In his book *Inside Gilligan's Island* he details the experience. I highly recommend it for anyone who might be thinking of becoming a writer/producer. Actors should read it. They would then realize a hit show isn't only because of them.

During the three years of the series, Sherwood took all the heat from the network. I had to ask him what was the latest stupid idea they had inflicted on him. His sense of humor never seemed to desert him. At least, with me. Maybe his lovely wife, Mildred, saw another side, but I doubt it. We worked on a set that was free from interference. We only worried how to make Sherwood's writing funnier. We succeeded with limited success.

The scripts we shot were polished to a glossy sheen. I remember going into Sherwood's office about four weeks before starting the second year of shooting. A pile of scripts was on his desk. Sixteen or seventeen. I said, "What are you doing? Going over last year's scripts to get ideas?" He said, "No, those are this year's scripts. Finished and ready to shoot." I thought he was putting me on. I grabbed a handful and sat down. Good thing I did that. They were second-year scripts and were ready to shoot. I couldn't believe it. In the three months I'd been off between the end of the first year and the start of the second, he'd been working, while I'd been goofing off. Saying things like, I needed the rest. Needed the time to recharge the batteries. Obviously, Sherwood not only loved his work, but the only thing that could shut him down was kryptonite.

I asked him if he had given the scripts to special effects and props. "A week ago," he said. This was unheard of. Those two departments now had a lead time of five weeks. The effects department was usually asked to do the impossible yesterday morning. Props was supposed to produce anything on instant notice. This time given to them meant that the shooting would be smooth sailing. "I've also told them to pick the ones that are the most difficult for them and we'll shoot them last," he said. When the effects department walked on our set to set up, they walked with their heads held high. They had been testing the gag for weeks in the shop. Refining it till it was perfect. When I flew, it was three times safer. When a hut blew up, it became funny. I'm sure it was one of the few times, if ever, these men were treated with the respect they deserved. It paid off. Say they were given three hours of shooting for a big effect—they could set up and do it in an hour. Perfectly. In one take. I still watch in amazement at some of the effects, which look so simple on the screen but are complicated and hard to execute.

Sherwood was a man of many talents. He even wrote the theme song to *Gilligan's Island*. How many hundreds of millions of people have that song stuck in their heads? Seriously, his most outstanding talent was his sensitivity for the feelings of others, particularly actors. He didn't treat us like children. We did a few pilots together and he would interview as many actors as his limited time allowed. This is grueling work. He was always polite and interested in everyone. When there were five to ten on the final list, I would read with them. It's torture for an actor to read for a part. I tried my best to put them at ease, but it was Sherwood who always came through with respect and support. He always cast the one I would have chosen for the part. In this pilot six actors were up for the part. On the day he cast it, they came in, starting at ten in the morning. One audition every hour. A whole hour to read a three-minute scene. I asked him, why? He said he liked to chat with the actor, put him at ease, talk about the part, get to know him a little. His office always had a warm feeling to it.

One time the network wanted their "input" considered in the casting. Each reading took ten minutes and the office was lighted like a dungeon. The man in charge sat behind his desk in the gloom, said hello, and ended with an insincere thank-you. Sometimes, he added the time-honored "Next!" The contrast between the two methods of casting was stark. The readings differed, too. At the network, they were hurried and flat. They never showed what the actor was capable of bringing to the part. The network was more interested in the actor's physical appearance. This was especially true for actresses. Sherwood, after getting the actor to relax as much as was possible, let him read as many times as he thought necessary. He took the time to explain the part and what he wanted. At the end of the meeting, the actor felt he'd given it his best shot. He thanked Sherwood.

One the day that casting had

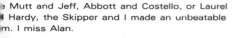

e Mutt and Jeff, Abbott and Costello, or Laurel
Hardy, the Skipper and I made an unbeatable
m. I miss Alan.

been completed, I went to Sherwood's office around five-thirty to say good night. Sitting in his waiting room were the actors who hadn't made the cut. A very depressed bunch. I couldn't think of a reason for them being there. As I stood there, the secretary's phone rang and she told one actor that Sherwood would see him now. He stood up and shambled to the office door. His face was a glum study of rejection. Fifteen minutes later he strode out the door, head held high, a big grin on his face, and bid a cheery good-bye to us. What was going on in there? I stuck my head in the door and asked Sherwood if I could sit in on the next meeting. He said, "Sure."

I sat as unobtrusively as possible in a corner. The next actor came in. Sherwood stood up and shook his hand and asked him to sit down. He then explained why he didn't get the part. It wasn't his acting. That was very good. The reading was excellent. He then drew a word picture of the qualities he wanted for the part. The actor could then see that he was almost but not quite right for the role. He perked up. Sherwood thanked him for coming in and said he was sorry that he hadn't cast him, and that he would keep him in mind for any future parts. What a pep talk. A coach at halftime would have been jealous. It wasn't phony praise. The actor left feeling much better. Even *I* felt better. I sat there and watched Sherwood do this with each and every actor. It was after seven when he was through. To take time to do this at the end of the day, when everybody else has gone home exhausted, only reinforced my respect for him. He is truly one of a kind. To find words to describe him, I suggest you pick up a thesaurus and look under the words *intelligent*, *kind*, and *humorous*.

Gilligan always had some imaginative casting.

GILLIGAN'S ISLAND: THE MAKING OF THE PILOT

Sherwood was also the only reason the pilot went to series. Ah, the pilot. I couldn't believe we were going to shoot it in Hawaii on the island of Kauai. It was to be shot in the third week of November 1963. We had looked at locations in L.A., and there were no tropical settings. I even went with the location crew on a boat to look at Catalina Island. It was brown and barren. Not a palm tree in sight. Someone said we could decorate it with fake palms, about ten thousand of them, but the cost might be prohibitive.

When they decided to look at Hawaii, I told a good friend on the crew, "Find a really beautiful spot." They were gone about a week when he called me. "Bob, we found a location," he said. "It's a little bay and it's more than beautiful." I don't remember the flight over to Honolulu, but we changed planes there. We got on a little puddle jumper to take us to the outer island. Kauai was dark when we arrived. The air smelled so good. We stayed that night at the CoCo Palms Hotel. It was lush. Right across the road from the beach. Palm trees everywhere. Lagoons and streams lit by tiki torches. The next day we drove for about thirty minutes to the location, and I fell in love with the island. That might sound weird, but I felt I'd come home. We wound our way down a single-lane road through a jungle. The warm trade winds were blowing, hundreds of birds were singing in the trees, and then we were at the bay. Huge breakers were pounding the beach. We all stood there for a while, just absorbing the scene, then some of us took off our clothes and went in the ocean. As I floated around, looking at the shoreline, I thought, this really can't be happening. I am one lucky dude. I'm going to be working right here for two weeks and they're paying me, too!

It was a joy to go to work. We had moved to another hotel to be closer to the location. The Hanalei Plantation was perched on a hill overlooking Hanalei Bay. The view was stunning. You can see it in the movie *South Pacific*. They shot the film right where the hotel was built. The rumor was it had been designed by two art directors from Twentieth. It was kind of like a set. The exterior was fabulous; the inner workings, not so good. It was the only place I've been where the toilet flushed with hot water. Bungalows, one after the other, went down a steep hill. The tram that was supposed to bring the guests up to the main hotel had lasted less than a year. It made walking up at night to dinner an adventure. Frogs were all over. Squishy ones. You didn't go to dinner barefoot, and not because of a dress code. My four-year-old son, Patrick, was with me and thought he was in seventh heaven. Just step out the door and grab one. He was invited to a real luau by the locals who worked at the hotel. No one else was invited. I wasn't too sure about letting him go alone, but by then I had realized children came first to Hawaiians. He would be more than safe. An old car came to pick him up, filled to the brim with grown-ups and kids. He climbed in, and as it drove away, his little face glowed like a full moon from the backseat. I was just getting to know the Hawaiian people and knew I could trust them. When my son came back, he wasn't even a little sunburned.

I was also getting to trust Alan Hale. When you do physical comedy with another actor, trust is the one essential ingredient that is needed to make it work. I had only met Alan when he tested for the part of the Skipper. We had been testing for weeks. Sherwood wanted a Skipper who could lose his temper with Gilligan, but you still knew he loved him. Not an easy piece of acting. We were doing tests on a Sunday, which was unusual, when Alan showed up. I don't know how many tested for the part, but I was close to giving up hope of finding the perfect Skipper until I heard this booming laugh. I looked over toward the stage door and saw Alan. Sherwood and I looked at each other, and I think we both knew, at that moment, we had found our Skipper. We did the test and there was no doubt. It turned out that we were testing on a Sunday because of Alan. He had been shooting a western in the wilds of Utah, and that was the only day he could come. When you're on location, the producer doesn't like for you leave for any reason. That didn't stop Alan, thank God. He got on his horse and asked a friend to ride with him to the nearest highway. He left his friend holding the horses and hitchhiked to Vegas. There he caught a plane to L.A. and cabbed it to the studio. He did the test and went back the same way. His friend was waiting and they rode back to the location, nobody the wiser. It's amazing how things work out sometimes.

After Alan got the part, the cast was complete. Jim Backus was to play Thurston Howell. He knew how to play the richest man in the world. During his days in radio on *The Alan Young Show*, he had created a character that was the forerunner to Howell, Hubert Updike III. Natalie Schafer came with experience from stage and movies. She did the pilot for the trip to Hawaii. She said that when she read the script, she knew it wouldn't sell and she wouldn't have to move to California. At the time she was living in a flat on Park Avenue in New York City. The "flat" was a huge apartment. She also had a house in the middle of Beverly Hills. Come to think of it, Jim had a mansion in Bel Air. Hmm, maybe there is something to typecasting.

Later, Natalie, "Lovey Howell," was vacationing in Puerta Vallarta when she got a telegram. She burst into tears. Her mother had been ill and the people around her thought the worst had happened. They gathered around her to offer their sympathy. When one of them asked if the telegram was about her mother, she cried harder and said, "No! The pilot sold!"

My daughter, Megan, and friends during the shooting of the pilot on Kauai.

The Professor was played by John Gabriel, a handsome hunk, and Mary Ann by Nancy McCarthy, who had done a *Dobie Gillis* segment and was the cute blonde. Ginger was played by Kit Smythe, a wisecracking brunette. They were all good in their parts and helped sell the pilot. Why, then, were they dropped from the show and testing started all over again? Meddlesome interference from the network. They gave some really lame reasons for the recasting. We started the process all over again.

I don't remember Tina Louise testing. She arrived from New York under the impression it was *her* series. With fourth billing, how she believed that is beyond me. She changed the wisecracking movie star into the typical dumb actress, proving that sometimes what you see is what you get. Dawn Wells was cast as Mary Ann—a perfect choice. A few years ago they did a nation-wide survey that asked, "Which girl would you like to go out with?" Mary Ann won twenty to one. I was sitting next to Dawn once, at an autograph signing, when a young man in his early twenties leaned over and whispered something in her ear. After he left, I asked Dawn, "What did he say?" "Thank you for getting me through puberty," she said, and we both burst out laughing.

As the Professor, Russell Johnson was more than believable. All the experi-

Bob Denver   Alan Hale

ments he did on the island were basically real. I asked him how he memorized all that gobbledygook. He told me he spent hours doing research in the encyclopedia, just so he could understand what he was saying. He seldom messed up those long speeches. When he did, we were ready. Shouts of, "Jeez, Russ, can't you even memorize the stupid lines!" and "Maybe we should shut down and give him time to learn them." Disgusted, we would all walk off the set. Russ just stood there, smiling, waiting until we were done. On the second take, of course, he did it word perfect. The new cast members were great, but I can't help feeling sorry for the ones they replaced.

One of the sight gags in the pilot was when Gilligan slides down a palm tree and lands on top of the Skipper. The director had picked the tallest tree in sight and had hired a Hawaiian to do the stunt. It was a long shot and all you'd see was that the wardrobe was the same. The Hawaiian wasn't too happy about putting on the white Top-Sider shoes. I could see why. He didn't need them. His feet were tougher. But he had to wear them. He went up the tree like a rocket, but coming down was painful. Literally. He'd slide a few feet and jerk to a stop, all the way down. His arms were all torn up from the stopping and starting. The director was yelling it had worked great in rehearsal, what was wrong now? He hadn't worn the Top-Sider shoes in rehearsal. Without them on, he came down the tree so fast it was scary. Everybody stood around scratching their heads. He had to have the shoes on to match when I landed on the Skipper. I asked if we had any white spray paint. They did and he got his feet painted. When they started talking about socks and shoelaces, I reminded them it was a long shot. If the audience could see he didn't have socks on or his shoes weren't tied, they would also see it wasn't me. I said let's get this shot or I'll never land on the Skipper. My double came down with his sprayed feet better than a fireman down the pole.

The effects department had the biggest gag of the whole show. Gilligan is surf-fishing when he hooks onto something so big, it drags him out into the ocean. The preparation for this started at the studio weeks before we left for Hawaii. I used to go over to the department to see how they were coming along. The effects man in charge was an old-timer. He had been at Twentieth since the thirties and had worked on all the major motion pictures through the years. He not only wanted Gilligan to be pulled into the ocean, but he wanted him travel all over the bay. It would be a spectacular shot.

It was complicated, to say the least. It involved three big anchors, quick-release shackles, miles of steel cable, a compound winch on the back of a jeep, and of course a harness for me. He showed me how it would work with a piece of plywood, some nails, and rubber bands. I would wear a leather apron from my neck to my knees under my costume. This was to protect me as I was pulled across the sand. The harness under that looked like a medieval night-mare. It went over my shoulders and had pants that laced up on my thighs. An iron ring protruded from the middle, chest high. A small piece of sheepskin went in the crotch to cushion you know what. I figured when I had all that on, they'd have to pull me around; I wouldn't be able to walk. The steel cable would be attached to the iron ring, then run through the three anchors and their quick-release shackles, then to the winch on the jeep. The anchors would be secured in the sand on the bottom of the bay. They would form a triangle. Buoys, attached to the anchors, just under the surface, would hold the quick-release shackles. Sounds confusing enough. Hey, it worked on the plywood board. The winch would pull me into the ocean from the beach to the first anchor. Then the shackle would free me to go to the second anchor. Same thing at the second and third anchors, and then back to the beach. He said that when he took off his hat, that was the signal to the man on the winch to crank it up.

That reminded me of a famous movie special-effects story. The effect involved blowing up the whole side of a mountain. Months went into placing the dynamite correctly, so the mountain would slide down into a ravine. There was no way to test this, so it was one take and one take only. The producers had allotted a whole day of shooting to get the shot. All morning the crew, on the other side of the ravine from the mountain, were making sure the four cameras would get the best angles. The effects man was triple-checking the charges in the mountain. The director was one nervous man. He went to each camera checking the shot and told the operators that they were to roll their cameras way ahead of action. If anything was wrong with the camera, get on the walkie-talkie fast and cut the shot.

In the afternoon, everything was set. The director was pacing back and forth at the edge of the ravine, talking to the ef-

You had to love the Skipper, Alan H

fects man. He stared the mile across at the mountain. "I don't see your men," he said to the effects man. "They're all hidden behind bushes or out of camera range," he said. The director asked how many men there were, and he said eight." Eight!" shrieked the director. "Eight! Are they all setting off the dynamite?" The answer was yes. "But we're a mile away from them! How will they know when to do it?" The effects man explained that each man had binoculars, and even right now they were focused on him. The director took a deep breath and calmed down. He looked at the cameras and the crews waiting for the word to roll. Everybody was tense. He looked at the mountain one last time and said to the effects man, "Oh, one more thing. How do you signal your men to blow up the mountain?" The effects man reached into his pocket, took out a big red handkerchief, and waved it over his head. "Like this," he said, and the mountain exploded.

I was smiling as I remembered the story and my effects man said, "Yeah, this should be a good effect. You're going to be going through the water like a bat outta hell." I asked him, how fast? He said around five or ten miles an hour. The ring on my harness was positioned so when the cable pulled me through the water, my chest would smash the ocean and I would rise up and skim along on top. I asked him, what if, on the off chance, I skimmed along the bottom? He said that divers with scuba gear would be stationed underwater at each anchor. I looked at him and said, "This is one complicated piece of business, isn't it?" He said, "Yeah, that's why I'm going over to the location two weeks in advance to set everything up."

While we were shooting on the beach that first week, I'd look out at the bay and see him and his divers setting the anchors. It was turning into a difficult task. The anchors wouldn't hold on the sandy bottom, and he had devised a way to nail them down. I didn't even want to know how this was to be done. On the morning we were to shoot this epic gag, I arrived early to suit up. I figured that getting the harness and the apron on, then trying to put my clothes on over that, would take at least an hour. When I arrived at the beach, there was a lot of frenetic activity on the bay. Three boats were racing around, dumping divers overboard and then picking them up again, only to throw them over again in a different spot. I looked around for the effects man and saw him sitting at the base of a palm tree, staring at the boats and divers. I walked over and sat down next to him and said, "Last-minute adjustments, huh?" He said, "No, we're trying to find the anchors."

I didn't understand. How could he have lost the anchors? He'd been working with them for three weeks. He said, "There's a large tropical storm about three hundred miles off the island. It caused the bottom of the ocean to surge toward the island. The sand buried the anchors. I can't even find one of them."

We sat there. I didn't know what to say. All that work wasted. All morning they looked. We changed the shooting schedule and shot some other scenes. Then one of the divers on a boat began yelling and gesturing. He'd found one of the anchors. The effects man was still seated under the tree. Dejectedly, he said, "Big deal. The whole thing is ruined. Can't do the effect with one anchor. I'm going back to the hotel." He left.

I really wanted to do this sight gag. We still had the jeep with the drum of cable on it and one anchor. I asked one of the divers if he could rig it up so the cable would run straight from the jeep to the anchor and then back to me. He thought he could do it. At least that way, I could be pulled out to the first anchor. We could stop shooting, reset, and they could pull me back to the beach. Not great but something. The only trouble was no one really knew how to operate the winch. That was to be the effects man's job. I asked my friend and mentor Ray Montgomery if he would drive the jeep in a straight pull. I trusted Ray. I knew if he saw me going under the water, he'd stop the jeep and back up to give me slack. It was a good thing I had Ray driving the jeep because that's exactly what happened. He pulled me about fifteen feet into the ocean and I didn't skim on the top; I dove toward the bottom like a submarine doing a crash dive. We tried it a couple more times, but the results were the same. Well, at least we had a tiny piece of the effect. I took off the harness and got dressed again and went back in the ocean to battle the eight-foot rubber shark. This was the fish that supposedly dragged me all over the bay. No wonder the gag hadn't worked.

When the pilot was tested for audience reaction, this sequence got the highest score. The people watching twisted their dials until the meter went off the screen. When I saw it, I laughed out loud. How did this come about? you ask. Sherwood. Who else? He took the original half minute of film and expanded it to a minute and a half. The wrestling match with the shark became hilarious. He did this in editing. He had the lab change the size of some shots so they'd look different. He reversed the action on some and made the action on others backward. The network liked it so much they used it for promos. I bet they didn't know the days of labor and sweat Sherwood spent creating that scene.

The SS *Minnow* arrived on a barge and was hoisted onto the beach. Looking at the holes in her, I could believe we were stranded on the island for good. That storm in the opening credits must have been the worst one of the century. I asked someone where they had got the boat, since it had appeared out of nowhere. It seemed there were no boats available on Kauai, so they had flown over to the Honolulu boatyard. The Japanese and Hawaiian fishermen were working on their boats when two men in suits and one laborer carrying a

Dawn, me, and the *Minnow* with its expens
produced g

large sledgehammer started wandering around the yard. This was a first for the fishermen. They knew something stupid was going to happen. All work slowed down as they watched.

The suits stopped at a thirty-five-foot cabin cruiser. The workers knew there was nothing wrong with it, except a seized engine. In fact, a few of them were saving up to buy it. With a boat like that, they would move up a notch in the fishing fleet. Also make more money. The yard owner showed up and the haggling began. Some sort of an agreement was reached, and the suits shook hands with the yard owner. They then walked around the boat a couple of times, looking closely at it. Then, they backed off until they could see all of the boat. One held his arms straight out in front of his body, his hands held up with the thumbs touching so a square without a top was formed. He looked through it. The other suit made a fist, held it to his eye, and squinted through it. All work stopped.

The suits then walked to the bow of the boat and one of them took out a piece of chalk and drew a squiggly circle on it. The man with the sledgehammer lifted it up and slammed it smack-dab in the middle of the circle. All the workers in the yard dropped their tools. And their jaws. The man with the sledge kept hammering away until a large hole was formed. Then, they walked to the stern and did the same insane thing. The suits patted the man on the back like he'd done a good job. A crane then lifted the boat up and put it on a barge. A tugboat towed the barge out of sight over the horizon.

The boatyard emptied as all the workers ran for their favorite bars. This story would be good for a couple of months and who knows, maybe a free drink. I'm sure it's still being told today. After I heard the story, I asked one of the suits, if there was nothing wrong with the boat but a seized engine and it was seaworthy, why didn't they just tow it to the location? The holes could have been made right there. He said, "You don't understand. The memo I received stated the boat was to be delivered with the holes, and that is what I did!" A budget for a show was always a mystery to me, but I was beginning to understand how the cry "You're going over budget!" came into being.

The *Minnow* caused one more problem before it was retired. Someone had dreamed up a scene where the *Minnow* is repaired and launched. I'm standing on the stern, saluting, as it slowly sinks out of sight. Buster Keaton had done this shot and it was hilarious. The studio sent their location men to a beach above Malibu and work was started. They were going to sink pilings in the sand and run track on them. The *Minnow* would be put on the track and pulled slowly into the ocean and sink out of sight. My sneakers were to be nailed to the deck so I wouldn't float away. A huge helicopter was rented to lift the boat from the highway to its cradle. Navy divers were ready to sink the pilings. On

Ready for a nap.

the day it was all supposed to come together, a park ranger, who had watched all this activity for weeks, asked the crew what they thought they were doing. They explained and he said no way. This was a state beach and that wasn't allowed. Well, calls were made to the governor and the park service, but the law was the law. Another $100,000 down the drain. The *Minnow* is now resting in a boatyard in Long Beach.

There was one night shot in the pilot. The Skipper and Gilligan are on the bridge of the *Minnow* during the fateful storm that wrecked the boat. The effects crew had built the bridge and put it on rockers so it could sway back and forth, simulating rough seas. Waves were supposed to be breaking over the boat and blasting them. To simulate this, a pump was put into the ocean and connected to a fire hose. A large piece of plywood was placed at an angle below the bridge. The water, being pumped at high pressure, would come out of the nozzle of the hose, hit the plywood, and spray up, producing a storm effect.

It was around nine at night when it was dark enough to shoot. The director said it was just one shot and that we would be back at the hotel by ten. The pump went into the ocean and we were ready. The crew member holding the nozzle was thrown back as the water came out. The force was so great he barely hosed the plywood, but he got some crew members. The director was yelling, "Kill the pump! Kill the pump!"They took off the nozzle and put two men on the hose. Take two. This time it worked great; the water cascaded up the plywood into our faces. "Rock the boat more!" yelled the director. The

crew obliged. I went out of the shot and almost fell overboard. Cut. Take three. The water roared from the hose, then trickled from the hose, then stopped. Cut. The pump had sucked up sand from the bottom and was out of action. For good. They spent an hour trying to fix it. Somebody suggested that the local fire department might have a pump. A driver and a jeep were sent to see.

We all sat around. This shot was essential to the pilot. The Hawaiian night was beautiful with balmy breezes blowing. I changed into dry clothes. An hour and a half later the local fire department from Kapaa arrived with their pump. They had a platform to set the pump on, thus keeping the sand out. It was now near midnight. For the next hour, they pumped and Alan and I rocked back and forth getting soaked, until we got the perfect take. I got back to the hotel at one-thirty. See how easy it is to shoot one simple scene?

I saw the pump problem one more time in my life. I was living on my farm, in Bovine Center, in upstate New York, when a neighbor's barn caught fire. The local volunteer fire department showed up and put their pump in the pond near the barn. This time mud clogged it up. The barn burned to the ground as everybody stood around watching. A farmer said that was "fittin'" because the motto of the fire department was, "we ain't lost a foundation yet."

Believe it or not, the last day of shooting was November 22, 1963. We were to move the next day to the Honolulu Yacht Harbor to shoot the opening. It was early in the afternoon when a driver ran up and said he had heard on the radio that President Kennedy had been shot. We stopped filming and tried to listen to the radio in the car. The reception was bad. A lot of static and fading in and out. The driver said he'd go back to the hotel and bring back a more powerful radio. Since we didn't know if it was a true or a false report, we went back to shooting. Only a few scenes were left. When the driver returned with the radio, we stopped again and clustered around it. We heard that President Kennedy was wounded and had been taken to a hospital. I think all of us told each other that it was probably a minor wound and he'd be okay. We continued shooting.

When the word came that Kennedy had died, we were all stunned. It had an unreal quality. Here we were on a beautiful beach in Hawaii. We all bowed our heads and said a prayer. Somehow we stumbled through the remaining scenes and rushed back to the hotel. Since there was no TV on Kauai, we all sat in the bar and listened to the radio. Having no TV coverage somehow lessened the impact and made the tragedy seem out of time. In fact, I never did see any footage for three weeks because I stayed on Kauai after the shooting was finished. When I got back to the mainland, people were still in a state of shock. All of them told me how they had watched their sets continuously for a week. That they had seen Oswald shot. The power of the tube was never more obvious. Everyone asked me where I was when I heard the bulletin. When I said on the beach in Hawaii, they all, every one of them, would describe the days of being glued to their TV sets and tell me everything that had happened. I guess it was their chance to get it all out. The whole nation was still in mourning. I hope I never see it again.

The next day the production crew flew to Honolulu to set up the opening scenes, but the shooting was canceled. It wasn't until the next Tuesday that we finished the pilot. I flew over and then right back for a two-week vacation on beautiful Kauai.

Sherwood, as creator, producer, and writer, was not so lucky. What he went through to get the pilot on the fall schedule was unbelievable. It would make a movie in itself. The first cut of the pilot was sent to CBS in New York. That version wasn't what Sherwood wanted, but his hands were tied. The network said no thanks. A second version, again not Sherwood's version, was sent. Same result. A third version was sent. Still not what Sherwood wanted, and the same answer came back. We were definitely not on the fall schedule.

Finally, Sherwood got his hands on the film. I honestly think that any other human being, by

departure from Dawn's girl-next-door image.
at's in that pipe, Skipper?

The Lagoon, where I spent most of my waking hours on *Gilligan's Island*.

this time, would have thrown his hands in the air and quit. He and an editor sat and cut and cut and cut until his version existed. Time, however, was running out. The film was smuggled out of the studio and sent on the last flight to New York, the night before the final decisions were to be made on which pilots would be bought for the following fall. After the final testing of Sherwood's version the president of CBS admitted that while he hated it, the audience loved it. It had sold. This same executive was determined to make *Gilligan's Island, Gilligan's Travels*. In his version, the Skipper and Gilligan would take out different passengers each week and have an adventure. Sherwood was determined to keep the seven castaways marooned on the island. You know who won. I assure you it was not easy. It was months of going up against the immovable object and eventually making it roll. Thanks to Sherwood Schwartz's persistence, *Gilligan* lives on.

After the pilot was sold and we had a time slot, the network worked its magic again. This is when they wanted the parts of Ginger, Mary Ann, and the Professor recast. Back to testing. For some embarrassing reason the network wanted the actors who tested for the Professor to do part of the scene sans shirt. You see, the double standard works both ways.

This recasting meant that we couldn't use parts of the pilot in our first episode to explain how we were marooned. What was left of the original pilot, after you took out the original three actors, wasn't much. We shot some added scenes with the new actors, but there was no way to complete a full show. The result was that the first episode that went on the air didn't explain anything. It just started with us on the island trying to get off.

The critics loved this error. In fact, the critics loved to hate *Gilligan's Island*. Some examples include:

"*Gilligan's Island* is a television series that should never have reached the air this season or any other season"—Hal Humphrey, *Los Angeles Times*.

"It's impossible that a more inept, moronic or humorless show has ever appeared on the home tube . . . *Gilligan's Island* are two words I vow never to use again"—Rick DuBrow, UPI

"Judging from the opening episode, there was some difficulty in seeing how far to make this one joke [?] go as far as one episode . . . *Gilligan's Island* would appear to have little future if the initialer is any indication whatsoever"—Dave Kaufman, *Variety*.

". . . Quite possibly the most preposterous situation comedy of the season"—Jack Gould, *New York Times*

"*Gilligan's Island* is the kind of thing one might expect to find running for three nights at some neighborhood group playhouse, but hardly on a coast-to-coast TV network"—Hal Humphrey, syndicated columnist.

BEHIND THE SCENES
OF *GILLIGAN'S ISLAND*

On the first day of shooting, I drove to CBS Studio Center in the Valley. It was one-tenth the size of Twentieth's main lot, but it was a hell of a lot bigger than where I worked on *Dobie*. I was waved through the main gate by Scotty, the guard. He was, and maybe still is, an institution in show biz. He wished me luck and I went to stage one. Yeah, there was my parking place, with my name on it.

The dressing rooms were attached to the stage. The big one at the end belonged to Amanda Blake from *Gunsmoke*. After all, the show had been on for at least a thousand years. Their stage was next door. Three years later, *Gunsmoke* was to play an important role in *Gilligan's* future. Basically, it put it off the air. The dressing room next to Amanda's was Alan's, then Jim's, Tina's, mine, Dawn's, Russ's, and Natalie's.

The reason I mention the order of the rooms is because, as you can see, mine was next to Tina's. I still remember the time I was trying to grab a nap at lunchtime when Tina was having sex with her boyfriend next door. Her groans and screams were so loud I pounded on the wall and told her to hold it down. She never heard me. Anyway, on the first day, I went into the dressing room and opened my closet to put on my wardrobe. The sight that greeted me was the same every time I opened the door. On the top shelf were all the hats. Hanging, all in a row, were the pants and shirts, and on the floor, boxes of Top-Sider shoes. Ray Summers, the same wardrobe man who had made the holes in Maynard's sweatshirt disappear, and I had spent a day shopping for the costume. We had agreed on bell-bottoms. The only ones we could find were dark blue, but we wanted them in a light blue, almost white. Ray said the laundry at the studio could bleach them out. For a shirt we picked a red rugby without a collar. He said the seamstresses at the studio could sew a white collar on it. The hat was a tennis hat, green under the brim. He said that it could be covered with cloth to match the hat. The Top-Sider shoes I had worn for four years without a problem. Since now I was a sailor, they worked. During the first year I went to see the ladies working on the costume, and they all gave me dirty looks. The second year all the clothes were made to order. Shows what being in the top ten in the ratings can do.

I put on the outfit and walked around the corner to the stage door and entered "Gilligan's island." The stage looked like a tropical island. A huge sky-blue backing at least fifty feet tall ran from one end to the other. Fake palm trees and real plants in containers created a jungle in front of the backing. Plastic flowers were stuck all over. Three huts, made from bamboo over steel pipes, were covered with palm fronds. Sand covered three-quarters of the stage floor. Up high, catwalks criss-crossed over the set and lights pointed down to cover any spot. In the first shot, the director wanted the camera to dolly back as the actors walked through the jungle. This meant digging down through the sand to the stage floor and laying track, so the move would be smooth. Two grips grabbed some shovels and began to dig. The normal depth for sand on a stage floor is six to ten inches. The grips kept digging. At three feet they hit the floor. The head cameraman, who had watched, suddenly yelled, "Everybody get out! This floor could collapse any minute." That was when I learned the first thing out the door were the cameras. We all trooped outside to stand around, waiting for the dump truck to come. Since it couldn't drive on the stage because of its weight, it was wheelbarrow and shovel time. That took care of the morning's shooting. Not

TV GUIDE

15¢

TV NEWS BULLETINS:
Too many and too soon?
SEE PAGE 6
LOCAL PROGRAMS · MAY 8-14

Bob Denver, Tina Louise
of 'Gilligan's Island'

We made the cover of *TV Guide* when the sh[ow]
first became a hit—no thanks to the critics.

an auspicious start. It was to get worse.

The outside lagoon was in a gully down from the stage, next to the Hollywood Freeway. Some mornings we couldn't shoot because of the traffic noise. Had to wait until the rush hour was over. The first day we went to shoot there, the director took one look at it and had a hissy fit. "This looks like a piece of shit!" he yelled. "It looks like the Mojave Desert during a drought! The fishpond in my backyard looks more like a lagoon! I don't care what it costs . . . make it look like a tropical lagoon. All right, everybody, back to the stage!" I have to admit he was right. It did look pretty bad—a couple of phony palm trees, some bamboo in ten-gallon cans, dead bushes painted green, and a big California olive tree.

So, for two weeks we postponed all the lagoon scenes, until it was dressed correctly. When the word came it was now ready, down we went again. The lagoon was more than ready. I've never seen anything like it. Every kind of tropical plant, bush, and tree—all in five-gallon, ten-gallon, one-hundred-gallon pots—were jammed together. You couldn't even see the ground. The whole hillside was covered. A huge palm tree was bent over the water. A noise, louder than the morning traffic, thundered in our ears. At the very top of the hill a waterfall cascaded down its cement courseway, tumbling over boulders and churning up the water as it hit the lagoon. The director shouted for the waterfall to be turned off and told me to go up the hill to make an entrance. I couldn't. The plants were so close together there was no room to walk. The director lost it again. "Listen, you greens guys did a terrific job, but make some paths for entrances and exits and keep that damn waterfall turned off. Okay, everybody, back to the stage!"

We shot for over twenty days and only had two and a half episodes in the can. You can shoot a cheap feature in that time. The network was nervous. They called the director, who was also the producer, and said they would like a meeting with him in New York. He went on the weekend. He explained that with a few days of shooting at the lagoon, a whole mess of episodes would be ready to air. The brass thanked him for coming. When he showed up at the studio Monday morning, he happened to glance at the directory in his building and saw that his name was missing. He went to his office, opened his door, and saw a new secretary. She had no idea who he was and asked if she could help him. He ignored her and went into his office. It was empty, except for cardboard boxes filled with his personal belongings. He had been fired off the show. The network had failed to tell him in New York. This, I found out, was normal procedure. An actress who was doing a series on the stage behind ours showed up one morning for work and walked onto an empty stage. Her whole set was gone. Just a few laborers cleaning up. She thought she had lost it big time. She went back outside to check the number of the stage. Yup, it was her stage. She went back inside and asked one of the guys what was going on. They were all scrambling to get out of there. She grabbed one and repeated her question. He suggested that she get one of the trade papers and read it. She did and found out her series was canceled. Cold, huh? That's show biz, with the accent on *biz.*

HOME SWEET LAGOON

When I finally got to go in the lagoon, the water was clean and warm from the sun. This was not to stay that way. It used to get so funky that one time we released a trout in it and five minutes later it floated to the surface. I said, "Hey, if the trout can't live in that water, I'm not going in it." The studio felt it was the temperamental-actor syndrome. It cost money to drain and fill that lagoon, didn't I know? I told them I would go in right after one of studio bigwigs did. I would provide the bathing suit and innoculations. They drained and filled it, bitching the whole time. They always had to be told to do it. Like, maybe, I wouldn't notice how foul it got.

If you think they were upset by that, it was nothing compared to when I asked if they could heat the water in the winter. Los Angeles *does* get cold in the winter. It has even snowed there a few times. They kept looking into doing it the whole three years we shot there. One morning there was ice around the edge of the lagoon and I asked the propman for a thermometer. He went away and came back and said he didn't have one. I said, "Come on, you've got at least twenty of them. What happened? The director tell you not to give me one?" Yeah, that was it. I said sneak me one, I won't tell where it came from. I put it in the tropical lagoon and it read forty-two degrees. I tried wearing a wet suit under my costume, but they only work when you're moving and generating heat. When you're lying on the bottom, the ice-cold water just seeps in, slowly. Since the wet suit makes you buoyant and you tend to float to the surface, I had to put lead weights on my chest to stay down. The only problem with that was, when I came up to do the lines, my lips were numb and I couldn't talk. Believe it or not, this dummy went under for take two. This time when I came up, everything was numb. The director said we'd try it one more time, and I said, "Nmuk foo!" through frozen lips. A grip handed me a styrofoam cup half full of brandy. Or was it half empty? I was shaking so badly, I couldn't get it to my mouth. I threw it over my shoulder and started walking, stiff legged, up to the road to my dressing room. I got into the shower stall and turned on the cold water because I knew if I turned on the hot, I wouldn't know how hot it was. When the cold water hit me, I jumped out, thinking I had made

Nancy McCarthy was the original Mary Ann. She was cute, blond, and a *Dobie Gillis* veteran.

that mistake. I was so frozen the cold water felt hot. It felt good. After a while, I slowly mixed in the hot. The steam billowed off me, filling the stall. I stood there, fully dressed with hat, until I slowly thawed. It took fifteen minutes. As I stepped out of the shower, there was a knock on my door and a voice called out, "We're ready for you on the set." Ah, the glamorous life of the actor.

The lagoon in the summer was kind of fun. The crew all put on their bathing suits and went in. There were platforms for lights. Any excuse would get them in. "Need help there, Bob?" Sometimes the temperature down in that ravine reached 108 degrees. In the winter, I was the only one, except for Alan. Of course, he always said, "What's the problem? It's not cold." I said, "Sure, for you it isn't. You've got a couple of inches of insulation. Look at skinny me. None!" He'd laugh that booming laugh, pick me up, and throw me in. While we were in there, I'd look at the crew, all standing there, wearing parkas with wolf fur around the hood, and shout, "Hey, how come you're not in here with us? In the summer, you've got lights on platforms all over the place. Look at that sun! It's dim and weak! We need more light! Get in a boat and get out here!" They always shouted back, "Shut up Denver!" They were never sure the director wouldn't make them do it.

One morning at around seven-thirty, I showed up for work and saw the camera was at the top of the berm, shooting down at the lagoon. All I could see were three outriggers. One big one and two smaller ones. "What's the shot?" I asked. I was told it was when the native headhunters flee the island because they're scared out of their minds. I couldn't see them. "Where are they?" I asked. "They're hiding in the jungle," somebody said. I looked, and sure enough, there were twelve extras in their native costumes crouched behind bushes and trees. Six of them were to man the large outrigger and three apiece went to the little ones. They had been told, no matter what happened, to keep paddling. The camera was undercranking to make them move faster, but they were supposed to get out of the shot as fast as possible.

On *action,* they ran to the outriggers and took their assigned places and started paddling like hell. As we watched, the big outrigger started to sink. The little ones on either side of it veered off at right angles to it. The water was coming into the big one, but they kept paddling. One of the little ones was headed toward shore. The other one was starting to tip over. Everybody was still dipping away. The big one slowly disappeared. The water was chest high and rising on the natives. The extras behaved as if nothing was wrong and kept paddling as their heads slowly went under. At exactly the same time, the little one headed for shore, smacked right into it, and the three natives rocketed out. The other little one flipped over, dumping those natives in the water. There was hysterical laughter around the camera. I've never seen a funnier piece of business. The timing was perfect. We couldn't stop laughing. I said we have to use it in the show, but we couldn't because the natives had to leave the island. Too bad. It was a picture joke that isn't seen enough on TV.

One time, when Alan and I were in the lagoon doing our usual antics, we had a director who did something he thought was cute. We really shouldn't have been out there in the first place. Alan's leg was giving him lots of pain, and I suggested that we put off the shot until it was better. Alan, of course, just ignored me and waded out into the water. We did the scene. He went under. I went under. We grappled and rolled around. The scene seemed to go on and on. We were out of breath and the director kept shouting, "Keep going! Keep going!" There's only so much you can do, but we kept trying. At last, we heard cut. Both of us were exhausted. As we waded ashore, one of the crew gave us blankets and took me aside. "I don't know if I should tell you this, but we're like a family here and well . . ." "What?" I said. "Well, the director cut the camera, and the last half of the stuff you and Alan were doing wasn't filmed." I looked around at the crew and they were all embarrassed. I went over to them and told them it wasn't their fault.   We'd keep it among ourselves and just let it go, for now. I didn't tell Alan either. What the director had done wasn't that uncommon. It's a poor joke played on the actor. Watch the dummies act themselves off. It usually happened when there was something wrong with the scene and the director lets the actors get a free rehearsal. This was different. It was plain mean. Nobody thought it was funny.

A week later he did it again. Alan and I were out in the lagoon, flaying away, when he told the operator to cut the camera. This time, though, the whole crew shouted cut. Yelling and gesturing that the scene was over. The director looked stunned. Only he was allowed to cut. Only he was allowed to end the action.

As Alan and I waded ashore, he asked me what was going on. I explained what had happened last week and that the stupid director had tried it again. It was the only time I saw Alan lose his temper, thank God. He started walking toward the director. A clothesline with dripping-wet clothes was in his way. He grabbed it and threw the clothes to the ground. They hit so hard, the water sprayed out. They were basically dry now. Alan was a big man but he seemed to be getting bigger as he approached the director. Bigger and bigger. The director sat in the middle seat of a row of director's chairs, and people were leaving his vicinity in a hurry. He sat there all alone. Everybody somehow knew what Alan was going to do. He was going to pick up the chair by the arms, with the director in it, and throw it in the lagoon. He bent over and took hold and then took a deep breath. And stopped. With his face about three inches away from the director's, he started talking to him. The director was white. We couldn't hear what Alan was saying because none of us wanted to be that close to the action. He stood up and walked away. The director sat there, limp. He knew how close he had come to being physically damaged. I asked Alan what he had said to him. He said, "I told him to never try that again." He didn't even have to say "or else."

So many sight gags were done at the lagoon it's hard to pick a favorite. In the first few weeks of shooting they hired a stuntman to do some of my physical work. The first one he did was to slide down from the top of the lagoon, down a trench, into the lagoon. The trench was lined with brown plastic and water was run down it. A very long, slippery slide. He went down it for the long shot and, at one of the turns, shot off into the bushes. They banked that turn and he did it again. Then it was my turn for the medium shot, so you could see it was really me. I started at the top and was supposed to go ten feet, then stop. Who's kidding who? I zipped straight to the bottom and plunged into the lagoon. It was fun. Like the luge without a sled.

Then I went back to the middle of the hill and did it again. I then realized I had done what the stuntman had been hired to do. Only I did it four times, at least. From then on, I let the stuntman do the gag first, so he could get paid, and then

I would do it. Except for high falls. He was welcome to those. They changed the end of the slide from the lagoon to a mud pit. A small hill of dirt was built to simulate the last part of the slide, and a six-foot hole was dug at the bottom. When I arrived at the location, they were filling it with stuff from fifty-gallon drums. I didn't know mud came ready-made. I looked closely at the drums, and on the side, in big letters, was the word OATMEAL. Quarts of brown food coloring were being poured into the pit. A fire hose was churning the whole mess up. What was going on? It turned out that real mud was too dense for the stunt to work. I was supposed to go under and disappear.

When I went under, it was the most complete silence I had ever heard. I couldn't hear cut, so I stayed under as long as I could, then shot to the surface. Someone pulled me out and I was hosed down until I could see and hear again. On the second take, I took a real big deep breath as I came off the hill and went into the oatmeal. I held my breath and stayed on the bottom and waited. And waited, thinking the crew would panic and somebody would think I was in trouble and jump in to save me. I finally came up and got hosed off and asked why no one had come to the rescue. They all looked at me and said, "You pulled that gag too many times on us in the lagoon. No way we'd fall for it here!" They were right. I had got some of them to dive into the lagoon on the same pretext. These guys were getting too sharp.

The lagoon was our location. I got to know it intimately. While it was mostly fun, I don't miss it. But enough of the lagoon, let's talk about my friends.

THE CAST(AWAYS)

ALAN HALE

Working with Alan was a joy. He was a pure professional. Always knew his lines and was capable of improvising at the last minute. Many times, just before the take, we would whisper to each other what we were going to do in the scene. No rehearsal, we trusted each other. Every once in a while, we would get a crew member to burst out laughing, ruining the take. This is the highest compliment. We knew the audience at home watching would laugh, too.

Alan also loved to tell long and involved stories with the corniest possible punch line. For the first few months he caught me. I'd listen to the story for ten minutes, then he'd give the god-awful punch line. I finally learned to look deep into his eyes, and if I saw the tiny twinkle in there, I split.

How bad were they? Listen to this. One morning, he came on the set and said that he had seen a car wreck coming to the studio. The story went on for

twenty minutes. He had ten people listening. They even waited while he went and did a scene. The cars in the accident were a Pinto and a Falcon. After describing the fire engines that were there and the ambulances, he had everybody nodding somberly. Then he let them have it: "There was horseshit and feathers all over the road!" Then he walked away, booming out his great laugh. They stood there and looked at me with blank faces. I took off.

He also told straight jokes that were funny. His repertoire ran out after two years. He and Jim had a contest those two years telling jokes. I have never laughed that much. When Jim ran out, he had friends in New York call him at six in the morning with a new joke, just so he could tell it before Alan heard it.

As I look back on those years working with Alan, I realize more and more, it was a special time. We had great fun together and he made the work seem easy. He brings a smile to my face even now.

JIM BACKUS

What can I say about Jim? When Alan didn't have me laughing, Jim did. When he arrived on the set, the jokes started, and they were good ones. One of the things I liked about him was that he was always up. Full of energy. One of his favorite things to do involved the soundman. When he exited a hut, he did what he called "mumble offs." With his back to the camera he would mumble a bunch of words in a low voice. The content was sometimes rated triple X. We'd have to stop shooting and ask the soundman to play it back. I'd say to Jim, "Come on, this is a family show!" He'd just laugh.

Jim had a long acting career and it wasn't all comedy. Most notable was the film *Rebel Without a Cause* where he costarred with James Dean. Of course, everyone remembers him as the voice of nearsighted Mr. Magoo. During the series, he put an act together for Vegas with him playing Mr. Magoo. He also took the gorilla from the show with him. He showed up one day made up as Mr. Magoo. It was scary. He looked exactly like the cartoon character. I still have one of the rubber noses he wore.

Jim had a great sense of humor and perspective about the show, its silliness, and the fact that its astounding popularity drove the critics crazy. Once, after he was bit by the macaw on the set of the show, he did express some second thoughts about Gilligan-mania: "Sometimes in the silence of my lonely room, I [know] I would like to do something maybe a little more worthwhile or artistically satisfying. But I enjoy the money and I certainly enjoy the recognition."

Jim also wrote several books, including *Backus Strikes Back,* which tells of his battle with Parkinson's disease. It finally got him, but he was a trouper all the way.

Natalie Schafer

Natalie was a hoot. She was the perfect Lovey Howell. She was another actor who was always prepared. This was no surprise because she had twenty-five years of appearing on Broadway, plus numerous film credits. *The Time of Your Life, The Snake Pit, 40 Carats,* to name a few. We'd rehearse a scene a couple of times and then shoot it. For Natalie it was all the same. She gave her all. Many times, after the scene was filmed, she would ask, ''Was that a take?'' We would tell her yes and she would say, ''Oh, good!'' She had a great sense of humor, proven by the fact that she picked out all the clothes Lovey Howell wore.

We couldn't wait to see what outrageous outfit she'd wear. Her lorgnettes were not only a prop, she also used them to see. One time we had a real ugly monkey on the set and the trainer had brought him in all wrapped up in baby blankets. I was holding the monkey when Natalie looked over and said, ''Oh, Bob, another baby? Don't you know when to stop?'' She came over and asked if she could have a look at the new addition to the Denver clan. I said, ''Sure,'' and she leaned over with the lorgnette poised to get a good look. I flipped back the blanket and she was nose to nose with the monkey. She screamed and leaped back, causing the lorgnette to fly out of her hand into the jungle. The propman never found it.

We never knew Natalie's age. She refused to tell us. I said to her, ''You have to tell the doctor who examines you for the insurance on the show, so why not tell us?'' She said, ''When he asks me my age, I tell him to look up what it says on the last examination.'' When the doctor tried to do this, he ran into a blank wall because that is what Natalie always said to the doctors, from the beginning of her career. When we were shooting the third Gilligan movie, fifteen years had passed, but Natalie looked and

and Natalie were the quintessence of class.

acted the same. In one scene, she was asked to jump and bounce around like a teenage cheerleader. She did a great job. Who would have guessed she was in her eighties at the time? It was only after she passed away that her real age was revealed. I hope I end up the same way.

DAWN WELLS

Dawn *was* Mary Ann. She tested for the part against the likes of Raquel Welch and won hands down. She's a very good actress, who has been typecast like the rest of us, but that hasn't stopped her from doing the national tour of *They're Playing My Song* and appearing on stage all over this country for the past twenty-five years. Working with her over the past twenty-nine years has shown me what a kind, intelligent, and energetic person she is. We joke we'll be doing Gilligan and Mary Ann when we're ninety years old.

One fan told Dawn Wells that she was the only thing that got him through puberty.

When there was a scene with just Dawn and me, a problem always arose. Sherwood would write three minutes of dialogue and we would do it in forty-five seconds. We really talked fast. The script girl was forever going to the phone and calling Sherwood and saying, "They did it again! Better send down some more pages or the show will be short."

Dawn knew well that the biggest fans of the show were kids who loved the cartoonlike plots. Way back during the first season, she told a story about someone who didn't listen to the critics. "I have a little three-and-a-half-year-old neighbor who told me every plot of every show we've done. They remember everything. It takes a certain amount of intelligence to follow, but not much intelligence to analyze." I figure that now all of those three-and-half-year-old fans are about thirty-three years old with kids of their own. We'll be in reruns forever! And I couldn't ask to be shipwrecked with a finer actress or nicer woman than Dawn Wells.

RUSSELL JOHNSON

As the Professor, Russ did a superb job. His acting career started in the early fifties in movies like *Black Tuesday* with Edward G. Robinson and Roger Corman's *Rock All Night*. So by the time Roy Hinkley became part of Russ's

sell Johnson *was* the professor. If he was so rt, how come he couldn't build a raft?

life, he was an old pro. Lucky for us since he had the most difficult job of any member of our cast. How he memorized all those lines is beyond me. And he even understood what he was saying! I've always considered him the unsung hero of the show. He wasn't the one doing pratfalls and usually didn't get the funny lines, but without Russ and his portrayal of the Professor, *Gilligan's Island* would never have been the success it was. The Professor was the island of calm in the sea of silliness . . . the glue that held the castaways together. Russ's talent and professionalism made it all work.

The only time I saw Russ lose his temper was when Don Rickles guest-starred. Of course, Don could make anybody lose it. Russ had a dry sense of humor, which was great because the rest of the cast went for the big joke. Russ, Dawn and I do about two or three personal appearances a year. I always look forward to sitting with Russ and talking about the memories. My wife and I are proud to count Russ and his lovely wife, Connie, among our dearest friends.

TINA LOUISE

What can I say about Tina? Ginger was one of the sexiest characters on TV back in the sixties. You have to remember how different TV was back then. Remember how on *I Dream of Jeannie* Barbara Eden couldn't even show her belly button? Things sure have changed.

Tina came to the cast from New York and brought with her a whole "serious" attitude about acting. Method, motivation, Stanislavsky. Actors Studio stuff! Here on Gilligan's Isle!

She was pretty blatant about her unhappiness from the very beginning. "I was ashamed when I saw the first show. I had studied at the Actors Studio. . . . I only worked on things I wanted to work on in class, things like *Desire Under the Elms*. . . . I found I couldn't use my work at all in this show. It was quite a shock. . . . [The] show is like a cartoon. I wouldn't watch it if I wasn't on it."

Sherwood was astounded by her cranky attitude. "I would think she would be delighted. She's an integral part of a major hit. What else does an actress want? I don't know what would make her happy. It seems to me that she's not a happy person. I don't thoroughly understand her."

She never really got over being stereotyped as Ginger. She always thought it kept her from getting better roles. As it was, she went on to some illustrious projects, including *Day of the Outlaw*, *Armored Command*, *The Wrecking Crew*, *The Good Guys and the Bad Guys*, *How to Commit Marriage*, and *The Stepford Wives*. She still doesn't talk about the show much with any degree of humor, so I'm glad she got to do her "serious" acting in these fine films.

MY FIFTY FAVORITE
GILLIGAN'S ISLAND EPISODES

"TWO ON A RAFT"

This episode, aired first, should have aired second or third. Nothing was explained—how we landed on the island or how we lived. After the recasting of the three characters in the original pilot, there wasn't enough of it left for a full episode. The critics reviewed this show and had a field day. *Inane* was their favorite word. The castaways hear on the radio of their shipwreck, and the Skipper and Gilligan decide to build a raft. The girls give them leis of fruit. The Professor warns that there may be Marubi headhunters on nearby islands. Gilligan forgets to cast off the anchor and has to go back to shore to retrieve it. He then walks underwater to bring it to the raft. The Skipper falls in the lagoon trying to help Gilligan onto the raft. After sailing for three days, Gilligan eats the leis and the shark repellent. The sharks, of course, attack. They almost destroy the raft, and a tropical storm does the rest. Gilligan and the Skipper land back on the same island, but think it is a different one inhabited by Marubis. The passengers, seeing the smoke from Gilligan's rescue fire, come to the same conclusion. They hide in a cave and rig a trap on the outside. The Skipper and Gilligan go into the cave, setting off the trap, and in the dark a fight results. Everything gets straightened out, and Gilligan comes out dressed as a Marubi and scares everyone away.

While shooting this episode I learned how strong Alan was. We were on the raft and the sail was supposed to fall down. I had a little knife, hidden in my hand, so I could cut the quarter-inch rope to make it fall. We were shooting without sound, MOS (*mit out sound* is a term taken from an old German director and never changed), so I could talk to Alan. I said that I couldn't reach the rope to cut it. Alan, on the other side of the sail, said don't worry. I heard a grunt and the sail came crashing down. After the shot, I told Alan I didn't realize he had a knife. He said he hadn't. I looked at the rope and realized he had simply snapped it like a piece of string. I didn't think it was physically possible to do that. I still don't.

We went on location, for the first and last time, for this episode, at a beach above Malibu. The weather was lousy—cold, very windy, and overcast. The few palm trees that were brought for set dressing looked pathetic. Alan and I were to walk out of the ocean and build a fire with wood soaked with lighter fluid so it would light easier. But the wind kept blowing out the wooden match I was using to light it. By the third take, I was shaking so hard from being wet and cold that I could barely hold the match. I asked props if they could tape a bunch of the wooden matches together and stick it in the middle of the woodpile. They did this for me, and on the next take something like sponta-neous combustion occurred. The pile of wood burst into a full-blown signal fire. I thought, if the audience buys sharks eating a raft, this should present no problem.

So, in the very first episode, I went in the lagoon and ocean and froze my buns off. Not to mention the tank where we were on the raft. Onstage I had to be spritzed with water to match the shot from location. The propman had one of those tanks with a hose and nozzle that sprayed the water. He aimed at my crotch and let go with ice water. EEEyough! Good joke. He had another tank filled with warm water and soaked me down. I never got used to getting dressed in nice warm clothes and then getting sopping wet.

Tina told the propman that she had to have a parasol when she went out in the sun, and she wanted a twelve-year-old boy to hold it. She was serious. Was this a hint of things to come?

"HOME SWEET HUT"

A large hut is built to house everyone because a storm is coming. Gilligan, during the building, causes bodily harm to anyone near him. During the first night, fighting erupts and everyone decides to build his own hut. When they're all done, the Skipper tells Gilligan to collect all the tools he loaned out. As he does this, he destroys each hut, à la the Three Pigs story. The storm is coming and all go to the big hut for safety. The storm rages all night and the hut ends up floating in the lagoon. The Skipper walks out the door into the lagoon. Splash!

Ah, they could build a hut that floats but not a boat. The special effects department was in charge of the typhoon that hit the island. They brought in the biggest wind machines I had ever seen. Giant propellers encased in wire mesh, eight to ten feet in diameter, run by gasoline engines. They cranked those babies up and almost blew the whole stage away. Fake palm trees went

The "Wrong Way Feldman" episode was directe
the actress turned director Ida Lupino, who is a
to get a taste of the lagoon h

over, and the big backing rippled like the sea, only it was supposed to be the sky. Those machines could generate winds up to at least seventy-five miles an hour. The propmen had boxes of leaves and stuff that they threw in front of the machine. We were in the hut and didn't have to "act" frightened. Dawn was huddled next to me and asked if this was safe. I said I didn't know, but we were stuck until the take was over.

In this show I got to do all kinds of physical comedy. I could see that this series was really going to be fun to make. We were doing things that were usually only seen in movies. Not just one, but sometimes two or three big effects per show.

Ginger vamped Gilligan for the first time and most certainly not the last. Tina gave a convincing performance, but was she acting?

"VOODOO SOMETHING TO ME"

Gilligan is told to stand guard at night with the only pistol the castaways own. Not a smart thing to do. There are just two bullets left. He falls asleep standing up, and when the Skipper yells at him, there goes one. The Skipper finds him asleep again and fires off the flare gun to scare him. There goes the last bullet. During the night the supply hut has been broken into, and the Skipper, who has voodoo on the brain, tells Gilligan they're under a curse. He then stands guard with an empty gun and a rabbit's foot. He hears sounds from the supply hut and is attacked by something. The Skipper cries voodoo. Gilligan builds a rope trap and catches the Skipper and himself. These gags are "uh-ohs" because when you see Gilligan do this kind of setup, you automatically say, "Uh-oh." There were a million in this series. While searching the island Gilligan trips and slides down into a mud pit. Washing off in the lagoon, he sees a chimp steal his clothes. The Skipper sees the chimp wearing Gilligan's clothes. Guess what? Right! *Voodoo!* He takes off the clothes and puts his hat on the chimp. Gilligan sees the chimp and thinks it's the Skipper. The chimp is finally cornered but has the flare gun. Gilligan bribes the chimp with a banana, then fires the gun into the supply hut where all the flares are stored. He runs into the hut and it explodes. Amazing what you do for a laugh. The next day the chimp shows up with Gilligan wearing his clothes, and Gilligan falls into another rope trap.

Sliding down the chute into the mud pit was definitely like a D-ticket ride at Disneyland. Swimming in the lagoon was an A ride. The chimp was very young and easy to work with. For the first time I got to wear palm fronds instead of clothes. They are real scratchy. I also learned how to be pulled up by a rope tied to my legs. Very slowly.

The hut explosion was something else. I had to run right through the hut and out the back into the jungle to avoid being in there when it went off. Then I went to makeup to be blackened by the explosion. Then to wardrobe to put on my outfit that had been reduced to rags. I was then dusted with fuller's earth, which is finer than talcum powder and brown. I was a mess. I couldn't even sit down anywhere. We were behind schedule and the dinner break was coming up, so I told the director my problem. He assured me the take would be done before the dinner break and I could get a shower during it. I ran through the hut, way into the jungle, and it blew up. I went to makeup and wardrobe and got filthy. I went back behind the hut to wait for my entrance. The effects men would pop a lot of smoke and I would walk through it, looking like I had been blown up. The smoke went up and I waited for "action," my cue. Instead I heard, "That's dinner! Forty-two minutes!" I chuckled and thought, "Now, that's a good one!" I could hear the stage door opening and closing. The crew was going all out! Unfortunately, the stage got quieter and quieter until there was only silence and I knew it wasn't a put-on. I stood there not believing it when I heard footsteps coming toward the hut. The director called out in a soft voice, "Bob? Are you back there? Bob?" I sat on a box for the dinner break. There was no way to eat anything without getting dirt on it. After we got the shot and I took a shower, one of the crew handed me a sandwich, which I gulped down.

Tina was seen reading very heavy books on acting, Method acting guides. Stuff by Lee Strasberg and Stanislavsky. She sometimes said hello to us. I was getting the feeling she thought she was the star of the series.

"Good Night, Sweet Skipper"

The Skipper walks in his sleep and fights the battle of Guadalcanal, where he turned an ordinary radio into a transmitter. Gilligan falls into the lagoon. The next day the Skipper hears on the radio that a woman is flying around the world and should pass over the island. Everyone tries to put the Skipper to sleep, so he can show the Professor how to convert the radio to a transmitter and contact the lady pilot. He finally is asleep, but Gilligan falls into the lagoon and wakes him up. I'm losing count on how many times I fell in the lagoon. The Skipper shows the Professor the conversion, but it doesn't work. That night, Gilligan is put on guard duty (Will they never learn?) and hits the radio, making it into a transmitter, and contacts the lady pilot. He gets the Skipper and shows him how he made the radio work. This time when he hits it, all the insides fall out and the plane passes over the island.

This was Alan's show and it was great fun to watch him run with it. He was a very good actor and had a natural talent for making people laugh. I know now how lucky I was to have him as a costar. He always knew his lines and was always looking for ways to make a scene funnier. As a partner in physical comedy he was more than anyone could hope for. I could never hurt him, and like some big, strong men, he was always under control, careful, and gentle. I could run across the stage, leap into his arms, and all he would do was grunt and put me down.

I noticed by this episode the castaways had acquired hammocks, tables and chairs, and wooden plates and knives and forks. There were coconut mugs that had obviously come from a restaurant with a Hawaiian motif. Also a long bamboo table where everyone could sit. We used this table all through the series. I even carved my initials in it. There's a lot of time between takes.

Tina was tired of wearing the gown, so she had a dress made from sailcloth. Not an improvement. Sherwood still had to watch for too much cleavage. The network was very strict.

"WRONGWAY FELDMAN"

Our first guest star, Hans Conried, played Wrongway Feldman. Gilligan finds a propeller and with it, Wrongway, who says he's been stranded on the island for ten years. The Professor says he can fix the plane (he still can't build a boat!) so Wrongway can fly it to get help. Somebody sabotages the plane so it can't fly. Wrongway disappears under suspicious circumstances. Gilligan finds him and it turns out he's afraid to fly. He says he will teach Gilligan how to fly. He teaches him on a made-up control panel, with fruit used for the various controls. The next day, Gilligan is in the real cockpit, ready to fly the plane, when he realizes that he has to have the fruit to do it and jumps out to get some. Wrongway takes off and heads for civilization. Naturally, when asked where he came from, he has no idea.

Hans as Wrongway was brilliant casting. As an actor, he had credits up the kazoo. Every scene I had with him was fun. When he taught me how to fly, with the fruit, he had me laughing so hard, I fell off the log I was sitting on. As soon as the episode was finished, we asked him back to do another one. After all, he could visit the island as often as he wanted because he could never tell anyone where he had been. He loved doing the part. He felt there should be more of this type of comedy on TV. The director was Ida Lupino, a great former actress in her own right. Her credits went back to when she was a child. Stage and features. It was the first time I had worked with a director who had that experience. She had a great sense of humor and made the work "fly" by. We invited her back, too.

Tina vamped Hans and got turned down. I was beginning to see her vamping was the same whomever she vamped. Hans asked me if she was for real. I said, "Sometimes, what you see is what you get."

Hans Conreid played Wrong Way Feldman and wa
first guest star to visit (then leave) *Gilligan's I*

"President Gilligan"

While digging a well, the castaways realize that nobody is really in charge. An election is proposed to find a leader. The Skipper and Howell end up as the candidates. Howell tries to bribe everyone and succeeds only with Ginger. She in turn tries to bribe Gilligan but fails. The Skipper and Gilligan fall into the lagoon. The election is held and Gilligan wins with three write-in votes. All ignore his orders as leader. He ends up digging the well himself and building a lookout tower. Some leader.

This script was the first that was more driven by dialogue than physical gags. I only got soaking wet twice. Jim Backus had a ball with his part. It was the first time he really let us see Thurston Howell. He stomped around as the richest man in the world and I believed it. I was enjoying the other actors as an audience of one. All of them were so damn professional. I asked Jim how he had put such a lock on his character, and he told me that since he had played the same type during his early radio days, it was second nature to him. I also realized that we were doing scripts that were longer than normal for a half-hour comedy. There wasn't a wasted second. The story moved along at a very fast pace. So did I. I ran from one setup to the next. It was one way to get into shape for all the physical gags.

Ginger vamped Gilligan again. I could sense this was not going to go away. The only solution I could think of was to back up into a palm tree and knock myself out. So I did.

"Sound of Quacking"

The Professor says a blight is killing all the food on the island. Gilligan stands guard as scarecrow to protect the plants. He then falls in the lagoon as he catches a duck. The castaways plan to tie a message on the duck's leg and send it to Hawaii. Howell wants to roast it. Gilligan starts to train it for the trip. A note is tied to it but Gilligan has fed it too much to get it in shape and it can't fly. Everyone but Mary Ann now wants to eat the duck. Then there is a dream sequence in the old West. Actually, a takeoff on *Gunsmoke*. Gilligan wakes up and says he will kill the duck and serve it. Instead he serves an old shoe with feathers. Everyone feels guilty. Then, they see the duck eating the blighted plants and the Professor declares that it's okay to eat them. Starvation is averted. Whew! Gilligan sends the duck off to Hawaii without the note.

The lesson I learned while making this wild episode is that you can't train a duck. You can train a raven. With me as the scarecrow, the raven was supposed to land on my arm before I shoo it away. The bird did it during rehearsals. The raven wrangler took the bird and put him in his cage. He then

A typical Gilligan reaction

took another raven out of another cage and put it on my stand-in's arm, so they could light the scene. (The first bird had his own stand-in!) The stand-in also did the flying when a string was attached to its leg. He was a stunt double, too! The duck got none of these perks. In fact, there were a couple of ducks, all interchangeable.

The fantasy dream sequence was a first for us. I had done a lot of them on *Dobie* and loved them. We used the *Gunsmoke* set that was on the stage next to ours. I wore boots that had lifts that made me six foot four at least. The wardrobe was a takeoff on Marshal Dillon. We did the classic showdown in the western street. Talk about having a good time.

Ginger vamped me again as a saloon girl. The costume didn't change the vamp.

"GOOD-BYE ISLAND"

The Professor decides to repair the *Minnow*. What took him so long? The nails he makes either shatter like glass or explode. Mary Ann comes to the rescue. Her syrup for pancakes makes a perfect glue. The Professor and the Skipper start gluing planks to the boat and tell everyone to get ready to set sail the next day. By accident, Gilligan finds out the glue is only good for a short time. He runs and tells the others and stops the launching. The *Minnow* then self-destructs. Gilligan has saved the day.

We shot part of this one on location at the beach. It was the only place the *Minnow* could be placed when it fell apart. It was a special effect without precedent. Not only were all the planks supposed to fly off, the whole frame was to collapse. Cables were all over the place. It was done by the numbers and everyone got the hell out of the way. It was the first time Alan and I had a complicated physical routine. We had to get stuck to each other and the boat. We also worked it out by the numbers. Alan made it real easy. We got so tangled up that the director at the end of the first take said, "Print it! There's no way those two could do that again!"

The words *Mary Ann's pancakes* took on a whole different meaning. I could hear the crew, at various times, saying, "I sure do like Mary Ann's pancakes!"

Tina avoided the glue.

"THE BIG GOLD STRIKE"

This show was about greed. Gilligan falls into a cave while caddying for Howell and finds gold. Howell convinces Gilligan to keep it a secret to save the others from becoming greedy. Of course Gilligan buys this. The girls hook the life raft from the *Minnow* while fishing in the lagoon. The Skipper tells Gilligan that he has to work day and night to repair it. Howell makes Lovey work in the mine, then gets Gilligan to work at night. He falls (not in the lagoon) asleep under a table and the Howells volunteer to put him to bed. The other castaways become suspicious of this behavior and know something's up. They follow Gilligan and discover the gold mine. They spend a day mining but don't find any gold. Howell, naturally, won't share any of his, so the others start charging him for everything: $750 for dinner, $1,200 for six candles, wicks not included. The raft is repaired and the Skipper tells everyone there is to be no gold taken along. Uh-oh! They all get on the raft, shove off, and it sinks like a rock. Gilligan can't understand why it sank if no gold was aboard. He was the only one who didn't bring any. All say they have learned their lesson about greed, until Gilligan says he found a pearl in an oyster. They all rush off with greed leading the way. By himself, Gilligan giggles, because he knows there are only four oysters.

I think this episode was written to teach little kids a lesson. It was done with lots of laughs—the best way to send a message. Again, Jim played the bad guy, but you couldn't dislike him. I mean, his character was greed incarnate. Natalie, as his wife, digging in the mine was innocence itself. Seeing her dressed as a miner, with a metal bowl on her head and a big clamshell with a candle in front for the light, was enough to double me over.

This was the first time everyone ended up in the lagoon, not just Alan and me. It was nice to see the rest go under, but what a production! Men in boats with towels and blankets, cars waiting to whisk the wet actors away to their dressing rooms, and hair and makeup alerted to stand by. When Alan or I came out of the lagoon, we were handed a towel and trudged up the road to our dressing rooms. We wanted it that way.

Tina asked if the lagoon could be heated. Hmmm, not a bad idea.

"WAITING FOR WATUBI"

The Skipper unearths a tiki, which he recognizes as Kona, a native god. Whoever disturbs it will be cursed. (The Skipper sure knew a lot about natives and their superstitions.) An earthquake hits the island and the Skipper is sure he's cursed. The tiki must be buried. Well, it's buried and unburied, thrown away and recovered; it always shows up where the Skipper is. The Skipper falls into (not the lagoon! Can you believe it!) quicksand. He also develops a propensity for running into trees and knocking himself out. Copycat! Only a native witch doctor can lift the curse. Enter Gilligan. He dances around, throws dirt in the Skipper's face, and beats on him with a stick. The girls in native sarongs dance to a Watubi beat. Another earthquake hits and the Skipper believes he's cured. In celebration he runs into another tree.

Watching Alan run into trees was not only very funny, but you worried about the trees. To say he knew how to do physical comedy would truly be an

understatement. For a big man he was uncommonly graceful. When he was in the pit of quicksand, I knew my turn wasn't far away. I was again dressed as a native, though I had moved up to witch doctor. The only thing that made playing a native uncomfortable was the full-body makeup. The only way you could get all of it off was to pour a box of Ivory Snow in the tub and soak for a half an hour. Man, did that leave a ring around the tub! The crew had by this time decided that they were signing on for the run of the series. One of them told me why. He said that when he went home at night and his kids asked him what he had done that day, he really had something to tell them. Though half the time they didn't believe him.

Tina got to wear a sarong and nobody was sure there was anything underneath it. I sure didn't check it out.

"ANGEL ON THE ISLAND"

Ginger is depressed. She has a script for a Broadway play that she knows would have made her a star. To cheer her up, Gilligan convinces Howell to be the angel and produce the play on the island. The Professor builds a stage. (He still can't build a boat.) Mary Ann makes costumes and Howell directs. Gilligan gets to play a maid, a messenger, and a slave. Lovey Howell wants to play the lead, but then realizes the whole reason for the production is to bring Ginger out of her funk and changes her mind. After all, she is a Howell.

This was Tina's show and she ran with it. Sherwood made sure everyone in the cast would get his or her own show from time to time. What a sport. As the props arrived on the set, I could see that creativity wasn't limited to the actors. The phonograph especially—a hand-cranked version with the wheel from the *Minnow* as the turntable. It was becoming clear that whatever we needed would appear. I mean, where did those old 78 rpm records come from? I thought, we'd better not explain anything because once that starts, there's no end to it. As the slave I got full-body makeup again. Was this a trend?

"BIRDS GOTTA FLY, FISH GOTTA TALK"

This episode used the footage from the original pilot. It was also the Christmas show. The Skipper dresses up as Santa and tells the castaways they're really lucky, in spite of all that has happened to them. As Santa leaves them, the Skipper walks in with a load of firewood. Hey, was that the real Santa? I'll never tell.

Alan Hale was so realistic as Santa that members of the crew took their kids to the set to sit on his lap. Hollywood is a crazy town, but sometimes it is a magical town. Alan could capture the spirit of Christmas in the middle of August in L.A. on the set of a tropical island. Who needs snow?

I am in full body makeup in iting for Watubi."

"THREE MILLION DOLLARS, MORE OR LESS"

Gilligan interrupts Howell as he's putting (where'd he get those golf clubs?) and is challenged to a putting contest. A quarter is bet and the betting escalates until Gilligan wins $3 million. Everyone starts to treat Gilligan better. The Professor builds a fire for him (nah, I won't say it) and the girls cook him special meals. Howell hoodwinks him into trading the money for a worthless oil well, but the next day the radio announces the well is producing. He's rich again. Howell invites him to dinner, and the Skipper, suspecting more dirty tricks, goes with him. He won't let Gilligan gamble but gets into a game of pool with Howell. He loses $12 million and Gilligan is forced to give the oil well for the debt. The next day the radio announces that the well was just a buried oil truck. Everything is back to square one.

Jim was an avid golfer, and to lose to me even in jest really irked him. He kept trying to rewrite the scene. As it was, he never got to putt. I kept putting the ball in the hole every time he bet. He said it would be better suspense if he putted every other time. He was afraid the boys at the country club would tease him. I said, "Jim, it's just a TV show." He said, "For you, maybe." I think he just hated to lose. Again, the effects shop came through, with a roulette wheel and a pool table. We wanted to keep the pool table on the stage after the scene was shot, but the director said no way. He knew better.

"WATER, WATER EVERYWHERE"

Our spring dries up. Water is rationed. Gilligan is assigned guard duty to protect the last of it. They never seem to learn. Everyone steals water behind his back, and then he accidentally loses the rest of the fresh water. Everyone gets mad at him, so he goes in the jungle to sulk, but finds a frog, falls down into a cave, and finds fresh water. What a guy. The Skipper goes looking for him and falls into the cave, too. Are they a pair, or what? Mr. Howell throws them a box of matches, just as the Professor is warning them the cave might be filled with natural gas. Uh-oh! Boom! They fly out of the cave and land in a tree.

What can I say? The series was getting sillier and sillier. One day, when the cast was sitting around having just finished an episode, one of us said, "You know, the one we just finished shooting has got to be the most stupid, silliest one we've shot!" A crew member walking by said, "You haven't read next week's yet, have you?"

Dummies were blasted out of the cave in the explosion. Alan and I had to put up with all the bad jokes about how they were better actors, etc. It seemed Alan and I, instead of falling in the lagoon, had switched to falling into caves. Never gets too boring.

110

"SO SORRY, MY ISLAND NOW"

Gilligan thinks he sees a sea monster in the lagoon, but it's really a one-man Japanese sub. The sailor is still fighting World War Two. One by one people begin to disappear and no one notices. The Skipper wants to sail the sub back to Hawaii, but he can't fit in it so Gilligan tries. He sails it in circles because he can't read the Japanese controls. Everyone is captured except Gilligan and the Skipper. Gilligan sneaks the keys away from the sailor while he's asleep and frees the passengers. They all run to the lagoon and see the sub going in circles because Gilligan has the sailor's glasses.

Our second guest star was Vito Scotti. He is an actor's actor. His list of credits must be as big as the L.A. phone book. As a character actor he is

Vito Scotti played the half-blind Japanese sailor still fighting WWII.

always in demand. He can literally play any part. When I looked at the glasses he wore as the Japanese sailor, I broke up. They were three-quarter-inch-thick glass. I put them on and could barely see, yet Vito wore them and somehow got through the scenes.

His sub was made of plywood. Its "motor" was an effects man in a wet suit with oversize swim fins on his feet. When I was in the sub, going in circles, I would yell down at him, "More horsepower! Faster! Let's get this tub moving!" His replies were not repeatable.

Ginger tries to seduce the sailor but strikes out. If you're keeping score in the vamping marathon, it's something like zero for eight. She just can't seem to "score."

"PLANT YOU NOW, DIG YOU LATER"

Gilligan finds a treasure chest and with the Skipper's help tries to open it. They can't. That night everyone but the Professor, who's away on a trip, sneaks out and tries. No success. The next morning the Skipper hangs it from a tree, so that when it drops it will break open. Howell wants the chest for himself and says he'll play the Skipper a hand of poker to decide who owns it. The Professor returns and says a trial should be held to determine the legal owner. He will be the judge, the Skipper will represent Gilligan, and Howell will be his own lawyer. During the trial charges are filed and countercharges are leveled and then counter-countercharges. The Professor finally ends it and rules the treasure chest belongs to everyone. The chest is dropped and inside are cannonballs.

Real cannonballs were in the chest, and once again I was stunned at how strong Alan was. Two propmen carried the chest to a spot off camera so Alan could bring it with him when he made his entrance. They could barely move it. One of them tried to tell Alan it was really heavy. He just nodded. I went and tried to pick it up. It was like a block of lead. I suggested to Alan that maybe he should drag it onto the scene. He basically ignored me. On action, he reached down with his right hand and picked up the chest. He walked into the scene, swinging it, then threw it about four feet. I thought it was going to go through the stage floor. When the shot was over, I stood there staring at the chest with two propmen. One of them said, "What did you do? Take out the cannonballs?" I just shook my head. He opened the chest and there they were. There was a long silence. There was nothing to say. The two propmen, straining, lifted the chest and, huffing and puffing, walked away.

Ginger, the seductress, tried her wiles on me. I was saved by the Skipper. Didn't have to knock myself out.

This is about as sophisticated as we got
Gilligan's Isla

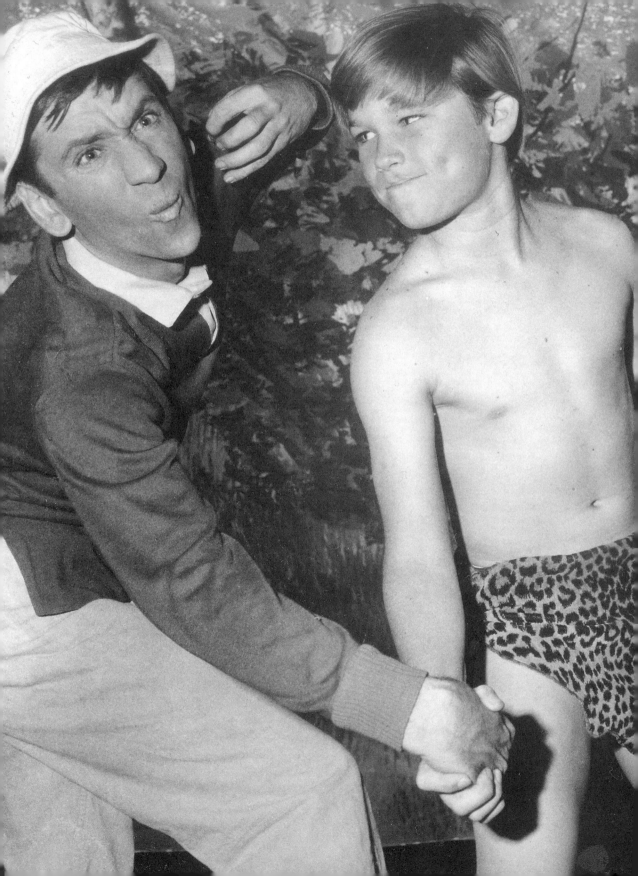

"LITTLE ISLAND, BIG GUN"

Larry Storch, our guest star, plays a gangster who has robbed a bank and hides out on the island with the money. How he picked this place is a mystery, even to me. How'd he get there? He cons Gilligan, but then, who couldn't, until the radio gives him away. Using Mary Ann as a hostage, he forces the castaways to dress up as natives when a rival gang lands on the island. They leave completely frustrated after trying to talk to the "natives." The gangster leaves the island, but only after Gilligan causes his bag of stolen money to be shredded in the lagoon.

The plot of this show really didn't make any sense. Gangsters coming and going, like we were a mile offshore, but it was saved when most of the cast dressed up as natives. Jim and Natalie were hilarious.

Natalie went for it. Black, fuzzy wig and full costume. She was a trouper. Never complained and always found fun in what she was asked to do.

Tina vamped Larry to get his gun. Also her native costume looked like an evening dress.

"X MARKS THE SPOT"

The air force is going to test a missile by firing it at a remote island in the Pacific. Its warhead destroys everything in a one-hundred-mile radius. The radio's batteries are dead, and it isn't until the Professor recharges them that the castaways learn of their impending doom. The longitude and latitude of the target island are announced, and the Skipper realizes it's their island. Mary Ann gives Gilligan two coconut cream pies because she feels bad about the way she has been treating him. She also gives the Skipper two, and he decides to give one to Gilligan. Uh-oh! The air force removes the warhead from the missile. Was Greenpeace around then? The missile lands in the lagoon and chases Gilligan around. It finally takes off across the lagoon and disappears.

While shooting this episode I learned that all the Professor's experiments were real. How Russell learned those lines is beyond me. When I read the script and saw the coconut cream pies, I thanked Sherwood. Alan and I could hardly wait to splat them in each other's face. We found out later that when the longitude and latitude were given out, an ex-admiral almost got a coast guard cutter, in Hawaii, to steam out to rescue us. Fortunately, a young sailor told the captain he thought it was a TV show.

Tina didn't vamp anyone! I think it was a first!

"GILLIGAN MEETS JUNGLE BOY"

Gilligan finds a jungle boy in the jungle. Where else? The boy was played by Kurt Russell, who, I think, went on to bigger and better things. The boy shows

in his pre-Goldie Hawn days, Kurt Russell was
jungle boy found on our little island.

Gilligan a natural helium outlet in the jungle. The Professor decides to make a balloon out of the castaways' raincoats, glued together with tree sap. Still can't build a boat. Gilligan inhales some of the helium and floats around. The jungle boy takes off in the balloon and lands on a navy carrier. Since he can only mime, he can't tell where he's been. The series rolls on.

I don't see how we missed running into the jungle boy after all those episodes; the island wasn't that big. But mine is not to reason why, mine is just to fall in the lagoon or a cave. I flew for the first time in this show. I had my own harness made to order. Still, it does tend to make you speak in a higher voice. Sherwood told me later that some people trying to escape over the Berlin Wall used the same method of making a balloon. They made it. So, you see, life can imitate television. Or something.

"ST. GILLIGAN AND THE DRAGON"

The girls want their own hut and equal rights. Lovey Howell joins them and they move to the other side of the island to build their own hut. Ginger overhears the men planning to scare the women with a monster that looks like a dragon. The Skipper and Gilligan as the dragon try to frighten the women, but they whomp them with clubs and embarrass them. All the men have dreams involving the three women. The women think the men have made another monster and attack it, but it turns out the men are right behind them. The monster is a large weather balloon. Gilligan attacks it like a knight and lances it to death. The Professor says he can repair it with tree sap, but he needs extra fabric. Gilligan shows up with a stack of fabric, cut from the balloon.

I don't know what the Professor would do without tree sap. When Alan and I were dressed as the dragon, we told the ladies to take it easy with the clubs. It would have been better not say anything at all. In the first take, they barely tapped us. The director said it didn't look like they were hitting us. He told them to swing hard and pull their punches. I don't think the ladies had ever thrown a punch, much less pulled one. On the second take, they let us have it. Alan and I ruined that take by throwing off the dragon costume and yelling, "Stop it! Ow! Stop it. Ooooh! Stop it! Son of a gun!" I don't know how it happened, but when the women rejoined the men, the equal rights thing was forgotten. Maybe beating us up solved it.

"BIG MAN ON A LITTLE STICK"

A surfer rides a giant tidal wave from Honolulu to the island. Denny ("Tarzan") Miller played the surfer. The girls fall for him hard, you know. And dude, the men are jealous and start working out. A hopeless case, man. Duke, the surfer, decides not to leave the island, not with Mary Ann and Ginger around. Howell has a plan, though. When Duke goes to woo Ginger, he sees her kissing the Professor, and when he goes to see Mary Ann, she's kissing Gilligan. The next day, he catches a reverse tidal wave back to Hawaii, hits his head on some rocks, and can't remember where he's been. So what else is new?

Denny Miller was a real surfer. I don't think the girls had to act real hard to be attracted to him. This was one of the premises that Sherwood told me about when I first met him. It turned out even funnier than I'd expected. It's one of the fans' favorites. Tina didn't really come on to him, but he tried to seduce her. She turns him down. What's going on here?

"DIAMONDS ARE AN APE'S BEST FRIEND"

Gilligan sees a gorilla, but the Skipper doesn't believe him. The gorilla steals Mrs. Howell's brooch and then her, taking her to a cave. Trying to rescue her, Howell gets chased away and the Skipper gets thrown over the gorilla's head. Gilligan makes a net and captures the Professor and the Skipper. The ape is attracted to perfume, and Gilligan douses himself with some. The gorilla runs off with Gilligan, freeing Mrs. Howell. Later, Gilligan returns and says the gorilla found a mate and let him go.

Janos Prohaska played the gorilla, or should I say, became the gorilla. He owned the gorilla costume, and when he put it on, Janos disappeared. I'd talk to him and only get gorilla grunts in return. He wasn't a big man, more like five foot four, and I wondered if he would be able to hold on to me as he swung from vine to vine. He was a former Hungarian acrobat and I shouldn't have worried. He swooped over to me, latched on, and swung off to another tree. When he grabbed me, his arms felt like steel cables, and I felt not only safe but couldn't breathe. It was kind of weird working with him. With the gorilla suit on and Janos gone, it was similar to working with a real gorilla. The suit was so hot to wear that when he took it off, he looked like he had just stepped out of the shower. He once took off his gorilla foot and poured out about a half a glass of "water." He was a sweet man when he wasn't in the suit. As the gorilla he was reasonably safe, but as the chimp, look out.

Ginger tried to lure the gorilla. That's a switch. I guess if it walked and didn't even talk, it was fair game.

"HOW TO BE A HERO"

Gilligan tries to save Mary Ann from drowning and is pulled under. The Skipper saves them both and becomes a hero. Gilligan thinks he's a failure. A headhunter is loose on the island. The Skipper fakes being pinned under a log so

Gilligan can rescue him and be a hero, too. Gilligan drops the log on both of them. The Professor and the girls lift the log and free them. The headhunter starts to hunt heads. Gilligan overhears the Skipper tell the girls that he'll dress up as a headhunter and capture the girls and then let Gilligan rescue them. The real headhunter, meanwhile, captures everybody but the Skipper and Gilligan. Gilligan stumbles onto the real headhunter and his captives and, thinking it's the Skipper, gets him to run into a tree and knock himself out. He returns to find the Skipper dressed as a headhunter (I don't know about you, but I'm getting confused); then the real headhunter runs in and Gilligan pushes him into the fire, thus becoming a hero. Whew! Oh, the real headhunter runs to the lagoon and swims away. After explaining this episode, I realize this ranks up there as the all-time most complicated plot Sherwood ever wrote.

"THE RETURN OF WRONGWAY FELDMAN"

Wrongway (Hans Conried) returns to the island and tells the castaways that he didn't tell anybody where the island was because he's fleeing civilization and is going to live on the island. Everyone tries to get him to leave. Gilligan fakes a fever and Wrongway takes off for Hawaii. He returns with fever medicine. The group decides to make living on the island unbearable. They start to civilize the island, driving Wrongway to leave. Instead of landing in Hawaii, Wrongway takes a wrong turn and lands on an island with hula girls.

It was great having Hans back. He did his usual great job. I think he landed a series after this episode and we never saw him again. Sad.

"THE MATCHMAKER"

Lovey Howell decides to try to make Gilligan and Mary Ann an item. Mr. Howell helps. A meeting is arranged and Gilligan kind of comes on to Mary Ann. The Howells reminisce about his proposal and then get into a fight. Lovey moves in with the girls and Howell with the men. The others decide to re-create the French restaurant where Howell proposed, to get them back together. It works. Now, Mrs. Howell decides to get Ginger and the Professor together. Mr. Howell is reduced to tears.

Over the years, the fans have always asked me why I didn't get together with Mary Ann. This was the only attempt. I wouldn't have minded, but it would have upset the balance that we had established between the castaways. Sherwood had a TV movie in the eighties that he tried to sell where Gilligan marries Mary Ann and they have a boy and a girl. The Professor marries Ginger and they have a boy and a girl. The Howells adopt three children. The kids then sail off to find the island and a new series is born. It

There was only one attempt to match up Gi
and Mary Ann. It didn't really v

appealed to me. Let Gilligan's son fall in the lagoon for a change.

Tina did a hula that was, without a doubt, the sexiest ever performed on TV. The hands are supposed to tell the story of the hula. I don't think so.

"MUSIC HATH CHARM"

Lovey Howell decides the island should have a symphony orchestra. Mr. Howell and the Skipper both want to be the conductor and have a sword fight with batons. Gilligan plays the drums and attracts natives to the island. No matter what they do to scare the natives off the island, Gilligan keeps practicing his drums and the natives keep coming.

I always felt sorry for actors who played the natives. I used to see them lined up for body makeup at seven in the morning. Two makeup people, with big sponges, would go down the line and wipe the makeup on. On cold mornings, you could hear the yelps and screams all over the lot. Then, the actors had to wear the fuzzy wigs that became hotter as the day wore on. On one show we had a lot of extras playing natives, and there was one guy who was never there when we needed him. On the phone or something. It went on all morning, waiting to shoot until he was found. The director wanted to get rid of him, and the makeup man said let him take care of it. After lunch, the natives needed their body makeup retouched. The makeup man took some warm coffee and mixed it with a ton of sugar and applied it to the extra. We were shooting at the lagoon. Every insect in the San Fernando Valley congregated there. Flies, bees, yellow jackets, you name it. We were shooting a scene with the natives in the background. I swear that on "Action!" every bug descended on

that unlucky extra. His arms were waving and he was bobbing and weaving. The director cut the scene and asked what the extra was doing. The director said, "You're just supposed to stand there." Take two was worse. The word had gotten out to all the bugs. "Cut! Sorry, we're going to have to let you go." The last we saw of him, he was running up the road for the showers.

"New Neighbor Sam"

The Skipper and Gilligan overhear gangsters in the jungle and then in a cave. They make dummies out of coconuts and bamboo and dress them like themselves, holding guns of bamboo. They hear the gangsters coming, and a parrot walks into the clearing. It says its name is Sam. Howell takes it back to his hut, where it shows great interest in Lovey's jewelry. When the word *jewel* is said, the parrot squawks and carries on. It leads the group to a cave, where it starts trying to dig up something. Thinking it's precious jewels, they dig and find a box of Jewel crackers.

Jim never liked to work with animals. The parrot was no exception. We told him he had a scene with the bird and he had to get familiar with it. He cursed a blue streak. The trainer assured him the parrot was nonviolent. He cursed some more. The trainer asked could he just perch the parrot on the arm of Jim's chair. Well, okay. Then the trainer gave Jim some sunflower seeds to feed the bird. This went well. Pretty soon, Jim had him on his arm and was acting like he was the trainer. "This is a great old bird!" he said with a Magoo laugh. The only thing he forgot to do was to make sure that his hand was always full of seeds. When they ran out, the parrot was fairly patient, then bent over and bit Jim. Hard. Jim exploded out of the chair, threw the bird across the stage, and started yelling and screaming. It was a bad bite. He was yelling he was going to get rabies, he was going to have the bird for lunch, he was definitely going to kill that parrot. He went to the nurse on the lot and came back with a big bandage on his hand. In the scene with the parrot, the trainer watched Jim instead of his parrot.

"They're Off and Running"

The Skipper loses a turtle race to Howell. He keeps losing. He then bets Gilligan's services and loses. Lovey tells Howell to let the Skipper win. Then the turtles get switched back and forth and still the Skipper loses. Finally Howell gives Gilligan back to the Skipper, saying that when it comes to Gilligan, the winner is the loser.

On the day we shot the turtle races I arrived at my dressing room at seven in the morning. I heard my shower going and assumed it was my stand-in. I got into my Gilligan outfit and it was still running. I opened the bathroom door and yelled, "Hey, you've been in there for twenty minutes, better get out!" As I shut the door, it struck me that the shower wasn't very loud. It was like it was barely on. I went back in and shouted, "You in there?" I opened the door and looked. Nobody. Strange. Then I looked down and on the floor of the shower were three big turtles. I carefully shut the door and went onstage. I asked the propman what the turtles were doing taking a shower in my dressing room. He said that they were in hibernation and he was letting warm water fall on them, like a spring rain. It would fool them into coming out of hibernation. And it did, but only for a couple of hours, then right back they went. All day they took trips to the shower to wake them up. I said, why my shower? He said he knew I wouldn't mind. He was right.

"THREE TO GET READY"

Gilligan finds a clear stone. The Skipper informs him that it is the "Eye of the Idol" that gives the finder three wishes. Gilligan's first two wishes are for a gallon of vanilla ice cream and he gets both of them. Everybody tells him to save the last wish to get them off the island. All the castaways gather at the lagoon and Gilligan wishes them off the island. A segment of the shore breaks away and floats into the lagoon. Gilligan pretends to throw the Eye into the jungle, and everyone runs to find it. He secretly pocketed the stone and kept it for himself. It's nice not to play the dummy *all* the time.

I think everyone as a child had the dream of being granted three wishes, and this episode brings back that memory. That Gilligan had the three wishes and didn't screw it up too badly is amazing.

"FORGET ME NOT"

Gilligan accidentally hits the Skipper on the head and gives him amnesia. In his stupor, he comes on to Ginger. The Professor says a second blow to the head can sometimes return the memory. Uh-oh. Of course, Gilligan, not the Skipper, gets hit on the head twice. Then the Professor hypnotizes the Skipper. He sees the castaways as children. He hypnotizes him again and they're Japanese soldiers. He runs off into the jungle, thinking he's still fighting in the war. He then captures everyone. Gilligan, looking through a telescope, sees navy ships off the island. The Professor desperately tries to hypnotize the Skipper but succeeds in making Gilligan and Howell think they are the Skipper. Gilligan hits the Skipper with the telescope and returns his memory. He bangs Gilligan's and Howell's heads together and the result is the same. Gilligan falls from the signal tower and gets amnesia.

We were in and out of makeup and wardrobe so much, we shot this show

Oscar or bust! Tina always hungered for much meatier roles.

on the side. First as children and then as Japanese soldiers. The only one lucky enough to avoid all this was Alan. He loved it. We'd all troop to makeup and he'd sit on the stage waiting, and then when we'd show up onstage, he'd ask, what took so long? Believe me, he had long breaks between scenes. Imagine the three ladies in makeup asking the makeup man to make them as attractive as possible as the Japanese soldiers.

Tina somehow managed to look sexy as one of those soldiers. I looked like Fu Manchu.

"DIOGENES, WON'T YOU PLEASE GO HOME"

Gilligan is keeping a diary and all suspect that he is writing nasty things about them. Everyone wants to read it, so Gilligan throws it into the lagoon. The Skipper starts writing his own and recounts the meeting with the Japanese sailor and his sub. It's pure fiction and makes the Skipper a hero. Howell and

Ginger do the same thing. Mary Ann finds Gilligan's diary and reads it to the others. It tells the truth and praises the others. They are embarrassed and treat Gilligan with dignity and respect. A *first!* It's only taken all these episodes to get there. Howell, the Skipper, and Ginger burn their diaries. Gilligan starts to burn his, but they stop him. He says it wasn't his diary but a book titled *A Boy Scout's Guide Through New Jersey*.

It was good to see Vito Scotti again as the Japanese sailor. This time we both stayed out of the lagoon. Hooray! In one scene Alan crushes a machine gun with his bare hands. It was made out of aluminum and lead to make it possible. I don't think they should have bothered; he could have done it with a real one.

Ginger uses judo in her fight with the Japanese sailor. It looked like an unfair fight to me. She towered over him and easily outweighed him. After all, she measured 37-25-36. I think the 37 isn't right. Still, it was the first time Ginger got her man down.

"PHYSICAL FATNESS"

The Professor is making a phosphorescent dye. Still can't build a boat. He'll paint it on a raft and send it out to sea. I suppose you've noticed by now that he's a great raft builder. The Skipper says that after they're rescued he'll rejoin the navy and take Gilligan along. He's split his pants twice and is worried about the weight limit, which is 199 pounds. He weighs in at 221 (oh, sure) so he goes on a strict diet. It turns out Gilligan is underweight and goes on an undiet. He eats the dye. What else? He lights up and they use him at night as a lighthouse.

Alan tipped the scales at 270 or 275 but wouldn't let us tell. One time he ripped the seat of his pants trying to pick me up and throw me into a hammock. It wasn't supposed to happen. I had read that if you could find any kind of leverage, you couldn't be picked up. Like a finger holding on to the shoe of the person who was trying to lift you. I tried it with my sons, who were four and seven years old, and it worked. I couldn't pick them up. I told Alan he wasn't going to be able to pick me up in the scene. He just looked at me like I was crazy and laughed. I went really limp on the floor and found the leverage. He tried and tried, then stood up straight, took a deep breath, and I knew he was going to grab me by the belt and collar. He did, and when he tried to heave me up, his pants ripped straight down the seat. Into the camera. Everyone broke up, especially Alan. He said, "Well, little buddy, you said you could do it, but how did you do it?" It was one of his favorite stories from the series. I wanted the shot to be used but was told no. I guess because Alan wasn't wearing the boxer shorts with the hearts on them.

"It's Magic"

A crate of magician's props floats ashore at the lagoon. Ginger says she was once a magician's assistant (uh-huh) and wants to put on a show. Gilligan runs around trying tricks until he overhears the rest complaining about him, then it's off to the cave to sulk. They try to get him to come back, but nothing works until they dress up as a monster. Mary Ann bakes a birthday cake, with flash powder on it, for him. When he blows it out, he is shot through the roof of the hut.

When I was doing *Dobie*, the cake gag was pulled on me for real. I got suspicious when I noticed everyone was ten feet from the table and cake. A blast of compressed air blew the cake in my face anyway. This time the blast was even bigger and covered the hut with cake.

"Good-bye, Old Paint"

A painter (Harold J. Stone) who has been on the island for ten years steps out of the jungle and introduces himself to Gilligan. Where the hell was he hiding? He says he has a transmitter, and to get him to use it, the group gets Gilligan to paint some pictures and then praises them. This is supposed to make the real painter use the transmitter to call some art critics. Instead, the painter leaves the island. He leaves a note that says the island isn't big enough for two geniuses. The funny thing is that he floats away on a raft made of old paintings. What gives? Why didn't the Professor think of that?

I'm not sure, but I think this episode was the first one without any physical jokes. No lagoon, no caves, and no pies. It felt weird.

"My Fair Gilligan"

Gilligan saves Lovey's life, so the Howells adopt him. He doesn't like it, but can't seem to think of a way to get out of it. He dreams he's a king and the others play various parts, asking favors of him. No one will play with him, so he orders their heads cut off. He wakes up. Ginger comes up with a plan to let Gilligan escape the Howells. He starts to give money away and pours a martini on the Professor's head. The Howells disown him. The next day, the Skipper saves Lovey's life and they adopt him.

I was supposed to throw a coconut cream pie at Jim Backus. Tina was standing about ten feet behind and way to the left of him. The crew came to me and said to hit Tina with the pie. I said, "Come on, guys, I can't do that. It'll look like I did it on purpose." They said, "So what? We'll get at least an hour, maybe two, off, while she goes to makeup, the hairdresser, and wardrobe. We can play cards." There was really no way I could do it, though it was tempting.

When I threw the pie at Jim, I twisted my wrist and put a curve on it. It hit him on the right side of the face and flew around the back of his head and went straight left at Tina. The crew cheered. I still don't know how it happened. They had the poker table out and we were playing cards before she left the stage. Her reaction was one of her better pieces of acting.

"A Nose by Any Other Name"

Gilligan falls from a tree and gets a swollen nose. He wants the Professor to operate on it. He does, and Gilligan wanders around with a clay head as a cast. He scares the girls and himself. A clay model of his face is made, so they can try different noses on it. When the clay cast comes off, Gilligan has his old nose. The operation was a fake. Later when Howell is swinging a golf club, he breaks the Professor's nose.

Alan and Jim were avid golfers. One day we had an hour break after lunch, and for the fun of it I asked them to hit some golf balls from in front of the stage. They always had their clubs with them. They could drive them into the parking lot across a gully. There were some cars, but they were real far away. They hit about ten apiece. Alan's drives were awesome. As we were going back into the stage, I thought of a practical joke we could play on Jim. I wouldn't say he was cheap, but I never saw him pick up a check. I told the crew that I would call the guard at the front gate and have him come to the set and say that a golf ball had broken a Cadillac's windshield in the parking lot. We would all agree that it was the sixth one Jim had hit.

The guard arrived and stopped the shooting, a first for him, and asked if anyone had been hitting golf balls into the parking lot. He did an excellent acting job. He said the owner of the car wanted cash or a check right now, or he was calling the police. We all went back outside the stage and looked toward the parking lot. I said I thought, maybe, it was one of those that Jim had hit. Somebody said, "Yeah, it was the sixth one." In a chorus, everyone agreed. Without a beat, Jim yelled, "It wasn't my ball! It was Alan's!" We all said, no way, it was yours, you'd better cough up the dough. The guard tried to collect, but it was a waste of time. Jim stuck to the story it was Alan's ball. He even gave it a number. It was the third one.

All afternoon we teased Jim. I would walk by and say, "You really should pay for that windshield, Jim." He would instantly scream, "It wasn't my ball! It was Alan's!" A crew member would stand behind and say, "Is that the police over there?" Jim would leap out of his chair and yell, "It was Alan's ball! Alan's!" Near the end of the day, I told him we were just putting him on. He took it pretty well, but said, "You know, it really was Alan's ball."

"GILLIGAN'S MOTHER-IN-LAW"

A native family is found on the island and they want Gilligan to marry their daughter. Another native gets into the act because he wants to marry the daughter. Gilligan and the new suitor have a spear-throwing contest to decide the winner. Gilligan's spear misses the native, but hits some coconuts, which fall and knock Gilligan out. The bride-to-be runs to the native and says she wants to marry him. Gilligan is off the hook.

Jim Backus's wife, Henny, played the mother of the native girl. It wasn't a great part. I guess she had been asking Jim to get her on the show, and this was his way of solving the problem. She had to dress up as a native, get the full-body makeup, and wear a bone in her nose. She never pestered him about a part again.

Eddie Little Sky, an American Indian, played the native who had the duel with Gilligan. He somehow brought dignity to the part. Ginger did her usual come-on to him, and his reaction was one of the funnier ones. He screamed and ran. He explained she wasn't exactly the kind of girl he could bring home to mother.

"SMILE, YOU'RE ON MARS CAMERA"

Howell makes Gilligan collect feathers so he can make pillow for Lovey. A huge pile of rejected feathers is in the supply hut. Uh-oh! A space probe, equipped with a television camera, lands outside the hut instead of on Mars. The Professor hears on the radio that the camera is going to be turned on. This is a chance to be rescued! Gilligan trips and breaks the lens of the camera. Time to make glue from tree sap. Gilligan brews a big pot of it and puts a lid on it. It explodes, covering everyone with glue. They chase him into the supply hut where the pile of feathers is, and voilà, instant chicken people! The TV camera comes on and the scientists can't believe what they're seeing. Gilligan breaks the camera again and everybody chases him into the jungle.

This one ranks high on the list of silly episodes. About two weeks after we shot it, I heard the network had a problem with it. They hadn't bothered us much after we got in the top ten, but maybe we had gone too far this time. The word came down. There weren't enough feathers on the cast. You could tell they were human. Shoot it again. We did. Still not enough feathers. All of us were getting pretty tired of this scene by now. It had been fun the first time. The third time we shot it, there were feathers stitched to every square inch of our clothing and glued on any piece of skin that showed. It was like walking around inside a pillow. The network finally gave it their okay.

"Quick Before It Sinks"

The Professor believes the island is sinking. A hut is built and put on a raft and called an ark. With Gilligan and the Skipper aboard, it is tested by the Professor. He rocks it back and forth until the whole thing falls apart. Of course, the island wasn't sinking; Gilligan was using the measuring stick to catch lobsters.

The fans like this episode. I think it's because of the scene where Alan and I test the ark. It reminded me of the silent movies I loved as a kid. My favorites were Laurel and Hardy and Buster Keaton. As the ark rocked back and forth, we had to improvise with the props. As usual, we couldn't rehearse the action. We ended up laughing so hard, we had to stop and start again many times. Doing the physical jokes was challenging as the ark was rocked more violently. We both got off that thing slightly seasick.

"Hi-Fi Gilligan"

The Skipper accidentally hits Gilligan in the mouth, causing his tooth to become a radio receiver. Gilligan wanders around being used by all the castaways as a portable radio. The Professor hears on the real radio that a typhoon is headed their way. What else is new? Gilligan trips and breaks the radio and at the same time turns off his tooth. Howell suggests that the Skipper hit Gilligan in the mouth again and turn him back on. He tries, but Gilligan ducks and the Skipper smashes his hand against a tree. Gilligan trips again and turns on his tooth. The typhoon is headed straight for the island. They all hide in a cave. Lightning strikes the cave and Gilligan's tooth is fixed.

It was weird doing this show. I had to wander around and open my mouth on cue and hope the sound that was put in later would match my reactions. I usually fell down in every show, but this one taxed my "creativity." I had to keep falling down either to turn on or turn off the radio in my tooth. Now I know how "the fall guy" felt.

"The Kidnapper"

A compulsive kidnapper (played by Don Rickles) lands on the island. He proceeds to kidnap Mrs. Howell, Mary Ann, and Ginger before he's caught. He arrived in a boat, but the engine is broken. The Professor fixes it. (Yeah!) Before the castaways can use it, the kidnapper escapes in it and flees the island.

On the first day of shooting we all waited to meet Don Rickles with a kind of dread. We knew how he could pound us with insults, and since this was *Gilligan's Island*, we were prime candidates. He arrived and we held our collective breath. He turned out to be a perfect gentleman. For the first two days of shooting. On the third and last day, having lulled us into a false sense

(Overleaf) Jim's wife, Henny Backus, got to ham it up as Gilligan's future mother-in-law.

of security, he started with the insults the minute he walked on the set at eight A.M. And never stopped until five-thirty that afternoon. It was an extraordinary performance. The insults just tumbled out one after another. To me: "Ya oughta take up boxing! Ya'd never starve! You're so skinny that when ya got in the ring, people would throw food at ya!" He had a field day with Alan's fatness. To Tina: "Ya oughta use your shoes to get off the island! They're so big ya could use them for pontoons and float off!" To Jim: "Ya know, you really look like Mr. Magoo!" To Natalie: "For a really old broad, ya ain't too bad looking!" To Dawn: "You're so sweet, if I was a diabetic, you'd put me into instant sugar shock." The only one he got to was Russ. I think he would have liked to hit him. For some reason Russ's insults became personal ones. They involved family, but then nothing was sacred. And on and on.

I invited Jim Arness from *Gunsmoke* over to the set. He walked about twenty feet onto the stage, and was hit with at least fifteen insults. He smiled, waved, and turned around and walked out. Robert Conrad from *Wild Wild West* did the same thing when he got blasted with, "You're really a midget, ain't ya! Those boots gotta have eight-inch lifts on them!" At the end of the day we were exhausted. So was Don. I just wish I had recorded all the insults.

"MINE HERO"

Gilligan reels in a World War Two mine while fishing at the lagoon. (More crap came out of that lagoon.) It's still ticking. The Professor tries to deactivate it with no success. He's been building a raft (I wonder how many he built?) and suggests that the mine be towed out to sea. Gilligan is, of course, elected to do this, but the mine floats back into the lagoon and explodes. Fish fly.

Bill D'Arcy, our first assistant director, made his debut as a director with this episode. He'd been waiting a long time. He had a great sense of humor and ran the set with an easy hand. We were all glad he was going to get his chance. He prepared the script weeks in advance. He had it down cold. The big day arrived and he showed up on the stage dressed like a German director. Beret, monocle, silk shirt, riding breeches, knee-high boots, and a riding crop. He announced, in a German accent, that there would be no fooling around when he was the director. When things had calmed down, we rehearsed the first scene, and then we were ready to shoot. Bill stood next to the camera and for the first time didn't have to say, "Roll 'em." As the *director*, he got to say the magic word. The tension was building. He took a deep breath—this was what he'd been waiting for all his life—and shouted, "Cut!" not "Action!" His nerves had got to him. He turned a bright red and we broke up. He left and returned wearing regular clothes and blamed the whole thing on his wardrobe. He did a good job.

"THE PRODUCER"

A Hollywood producer, played by Phil Silvers, crashes his plane on the island. He's on a worldwide talent search. The castaways decide to do a musical version of *Hamlet* to impress him and get off the island. The producer thinks the production stinks and proceeds to play all the parts until he collapses from exhaustion. He then sneaks off the island and produces a major film. A musical *Hamlet*.

As the producer, Phil Silvers yelled and screamed all over the place. He said that was how producers acted. I thought it was a little overdone, until later in my career. He was also part owner of the series, his company having put some money in the pilot. It still collects residuals to this day. No comment.

For those of you who liked the musical version of *Hamlet*, here are the words so you can sing along. The music is the "Toreador" song from the opera *Carmen*. The cast was Gilligan as Hamlet, the Skipper as Polonius, Mr. and Mrs. Howell as Claudius and Gertrude, Ginger as Ophelia, and Mary Ann as Laertes. The Professor wasn't in it.

[*The curtain rises. Hamlet stands center stage.*]

HAMLET

[*Sings.*]

I ask to be or not to be,

A rogue or peasant slave is what you see;

A boy who loved his mother's knee,

And so I ask to be or not to be.

So here's my plea, I beg of you,

And say you see a little hope for me.

To fight or flee, to fight or flee,

I ask myself to be or not to be.

[*Enter King Claudius and Queen Gertrude.*]

CLAUDIUS AND GERTRUDE
[*Sing.*]

He asks to be or not to be,

A rogue or peasant slave is what you see;

GERTRUDE
[*Sings.*]

My son who loved his mother's knee.

CLAUDIUS AND GERTRUDE
[*Sing.*]

And so he asks to be or not to be.

So here's his plea, we beg of thee,

And say we see a little hope for he.

HAMLET
[*Sings.*]

To fight or flee, to fight or flee,

I ask myself to be or not to be.

[*Exit Claudius and Gertrude.*]

HAMLET

Hark! I do believe I hear the fair Ophelia.

[*Enter Ophelia.*]

OPHELIA

My lord Hamlet is troubled.

HAMLET

Yea, verily, my heart is heavy. I cannot marry thee, Ophelia.

There is nothing left for you, but to get thee

to a notary.

OPHELIA

Ah, my poor Hamlet. Ah, my poor Hamlet.

[*Sings.*]

Hamlet, dear, your problem is clear,

Avenging thy father's death,

You seek to harm your uncle and mom,

But you're scaring me to death.

While I die and sigh and cry,

That love is everything,

You're content to try to touch,

The conscience of a king.

Since the day when your dad met his fate,

You brood and you don't touch your food.

You hate your ma, mad at my pa,

You'll kill the king, or some silly thing.

So, Hamlet, Hamlet, do be a man,

Let rotten enough alone.

From Ophelia no one can steal ya,

You'll always be my own.

Leave the gravedigger's scene,

If you know what I mean.

Danish pastry for two,

For me, for you.

HAMLET

In truth, Ophelia, you have said a mouthful.

OPHELIA

Hamlet, I have so much more to offer. But hark!

Me thinks me hear the heavy footsteps of my father, Polonius.

HAMLET

And the laughter of your brother and my friend, Laertes.

OPHELIA

Oh, they must not find us here. But where to hide?

HAMLET

Hide anyplace. But don't go near the water.

[*Exit Hamlet and Ophelia.*]
[*Enter Laertes and Polonius.*]

LAERTES

Father, my ship sails at the tide.

POLONIUS

A moment, my son, for I have something to tell you.

LAERTES

But, I ask only for my allowance.

POLONIUS

Ah, but I shall give you something far more available: advice.

LAERTES

Do you know how much wine you can buy in Paris with advice?

POLONIUS

Paris is a wild and wicked town. And you are but

a young and innocent boy.

LAERTES
[*To audience.*]

Oh, I could tell him a few stories.

POLONIUS

Heed my words, Laertes, and you'll be safe.

LAERTES

Unless I listen, I won't get my spending money.

So I'll listen, I'll listen.

POLONIUS
[*Sings.*]

Neither a borrower or a lender be.

Do not forget: Stay out of debt.

Think twice, and take this good advice from me,

Guard that old solvency.

There's just one other thing you ought to do,

To thine own self be true.

[Enter entire cast.]

ALL

[Sing.]

Neither a borrower or lender be,

Do not forget: Stay out of debt.

Think twice, and take this good advice from me,

Guard that old solvency.

There's just one other thing you ought to do,

To thine own self be true.

[Finis. Curtain.]

" 'V' FOR VITAMINS"

The Professor claims the castaways are suffering from a vitamin C deficiency. Gilligan has the only orange on the island and decides to give everyone a slice. A fight breaks out over who should have what, and the orange shrivels up in the sun. The Professor says they should plant the seeds. Gilligan has a dream based on "Jack and the Beanstalk."

In the dream sequence Gilligan played Jack and the Skipper was the giant. In order for him to look as big as a giant, we had to have a child play Gilligan. The search for a child who looked like me started weeks in advance of shooting. I told them right off that I had a five-year-old son, Patrick, who looked like me. They ignored me. I kept telling them. Two days before the show they came to me and said that they had looked at hundreds of children, but couldn't find one that looked like me. I said how about my son. They told me to bring him in: "My God! He looks just like you!" No kidding. He was cast as the little Gilligan. We drove to the studio together, and when we arrived, I noticed right away that the crew was going to have a good time with me. My parking space had been painted over. It now read "Patrick Denver." Same on my dressing room door. Inside there was a perfect little Gilligan outfit laid out. I couldn't find mine. Onstage, my chair had disappeared and in its place was a little one with my son's name on it. The crew ignored me and asked who I was and why was I there. The star of the show, everyone knew, was named Patrick Denver. He had a great time and did a real good job in the dream sequence.

"High Man on the Totem Pole"

A totem pole is found in the jungle, and the head on top looks like Gilligan. He becomes convinced he is a descendant of headhunters. In a panic, he lops off the head on the pole. Three natives land on the island and say that whoever did this must die. They capture everybody but Gilligan. He climbs to the top of the pole and puts his real head on it. This scares the natives away.

I had to have a death mask made so the head on top of the totem pole looked like me. This meant going to the makeup department on your day off, of course, and sitting in the chair for an hour or so. First the makeup man puts Vaseline all over your face and neck. Then he lays muslin over that. Then comes the plaster. It covers your eyes and plugs up your ears. You breath through straws in your nose. You can't move until it's dry, and if you get an itch, forget it. It's funny, but everybody says the same thing when they look at their mask: "That's me? You sure?"

"Gilligan vs. Gilligan"

A Russian spy who was made to look like Gilligan lands on the island. He is to gather information on the castaways, who are believed to be engaged in some top-secret work. He comes equipped with a Swiss army knife that has at least two hundred functions, even a laser beam. He knocks out Gilligan and becomes him. Gilligan finally unmasks him and he flees the island. No one believes Gilligan's story about the spy until the Professor shows up with the Swiss army knife.

It was my turn to do the "twin" show. You get to play two parts. Jim and Tina did one. So what happens? I come down with the worst flu I've ever had. It was the only time I was sick during the series: 104-degree temperature with chills. When you watch this episode, you can tell. I'd like to thank my friend and stand-in, Bob D'Arcy, for getting me through. The most difficult scene was with him and we did it in one take. How, I'll never understand. In a mirror gag, I think it's my reflection but it's the spy copying everything I do. I was too sick to rehearse and just told Bob what I was going to do. He duplicated my moves and made the scene. I went back and collapsed in my chair, wrapped a blanket around me, and thought how lucky I was.

It's a Bird, It's a Plane, It's Gilligan

A jet pack washes up in the lagoon. The Professor says it has enough fuel for one trip to Hawaii. Gilligan is selected to fly in it. He balks. A dummy is used instead. Not much difference. Gilligan accidentally (this *is* the operative word with Gilligan) knocks over the dummy and pilots it until there is only enough fuel left for a short flight. The navy is holding maneuvers off the island, so Gilligan gets sent up in the hope the radar will spot him. He hears on the radio that a UFO has been sighted, becomes frightened, and hides in a cloud, thus avoiding rescue.

I was hanging by wires about fifty feet above the stage with the jet pack when I looked down at two of the crew holding the rope that held me up. They were looking back up at me and asked if I was all right. I said yeah, and then they said to each other, "Let's get a cup of coffee," and let go of the rope. I screamed and thought I had fallen the fifty feet. But they had tied the rope to a stake in the floor and I hadn't moved an inch. My stomach had rushed to my throat and I had gone through the reality of falling. The mind is a wonderful thing. The two pranksters were laughing their heads off and yelling up at me, "You need wardrobe? Maybe a new pair of pants?" I said, "Just wait until I get down from here. You're going to be real sorry." I never did get even with them. I couldn't think of anything that would equal what they had done to me.

"SLAVE GIRL"

Gilligan saves a native girl from drowning in the lagoon. She becomes his slave forever. The only way he can free her is in mortal combat. Howell agrees to have a duel with Gilligan and pretends to kill him. He wouldn't mind having a slave. Three natives see the duel and one challenges Howell for the girl's hand. Howell wastes no time exposing Gilligan. To get Gilligan out of this mess, the Professor gives him a potion that makes him appear dead. The natives decide to give him their version of a funeral: burning the body over a fire. Gilligan wakes up screaming and frightens the natives away.

In the take where the seat of my pants was supposed to be on fire, I didn't have to act. The effects man used something called "liquid smoke." This is some kind of corrosive acid that smokes when exposed to the air. He put a rubber pad on my butt and told me the acid couldn't go through it. Then he came back and said maybe he should put a hunk of asbestos in my pants, too. I should have become suspicious by then. He took the eyedropper and applied the acid. Smoke poured off the seat of my pants. It was warm but not hot. As the scene went on, the heat increased until the acid ate through everything and finally reached my skin. Right in the middle of the scene I let out a yell, dropped my pants, ran to the rain barrel, and sat down in it. I had blisters on my butt for weeks.

"UP AT BAT"

Gilligan is bitten on the neck by what he believes is a vampire bat. He is

concerned that he's going to turn into a vampire. He sleepwalks into the Howells' hut and goes for Lovey's neck. He now knows he's turning into a vampire, so he locks himself in a cave. He then dreams he is a vampire. The Professor wakes him up and tells him it was a fruit bat that bit him.

Doing this episode was like being a kid again. At Halloween. For the dream sequence, I was made up as Count Dracula. Our makeup man was very talented and the makeup was perfect. I wanted to wear it home.

"THE FRIENDLY PHYSICIAN"

A mad scientist (played by Vito Scotti) comes to the island and takes the Skipper and Gilligan back to his island. While in the scientist's castle they hear a dog meow like a cat and a parrot roar like a lion. The scientist explains he can electronically switch the minds and bodies of animals. He and Igor (Mike Mazurki) then take them to the dungeon. The scientist then gets the rest of the castaways and begins switching minds and bodies.

It was very confusing to shoot. We had to go over and record the dialogue that the other actor said. When I was supposed to be Howell, I had to say the lines and make the faces like he would. The best was Mike Mazurki as Ginger. Watching him mince down the dungeon steps and try to walk the sexy walk made us ruin more than one take. I think this must be one of the all-time favorites with the fans. It's certainly one of mine.

THERE'S MORE TO LIFE THAN GILLIGAN (I THINK)

We were all signed up to do a fourth season of *Gilligan* when the network pulled the plug on our show. How this happened is amazing. We were still in the top twenty in ratings at this time. The fall lineup was all set, with *Gilligan* in the seven-thirty spot on Monday nights. When the schedule was shown to the head of CBS, William Paley, he exploded, "Where is *Gunsmoke*?" *Gunsmoke* was his favorite show. *Gunsmoke* was his *wife's* favorite show. "Who dropped *Gunsmoke*?" Well, nobody ever admitted to dropping *Gunsmoke*, and room was soon made for the boss's favorite show. Guess where they found room?

Sherwood called us all personally to tell us the unhappy story. After three years as one of the most popular shows, we were given the heave-ho to keep Bill and Babe Paley happy with Marshal Dillon and Kitty. That's show biz. It was time to try new things anyway.

THE GOOD GUYS

The Good Guys is the series I did after *Gilligan*. One in a thousand TV viewers has ever heard of it. It was on for two years, 1968–70, and from the first show it spiraled down to cancellation. I had two great costars, Herb Edelman and Joyce Van Patten. (In it I was Rufus Butterworth, a cabbie, whose best friend, Bert, ran a diner with his wife.) They were super to work with. The problem was me and the writing. We shot the first year on tape in front of a live audience. The writers loved it. The audience laughed at everything. It was disconcerting. You couldn't time anything. We went to one camera, film, in the second year, but the boat had sailed. I'd been doing series for eleven years and wanted out. Out of L.A. as well. I got my wish.

The weird thing was that we shot it on the same stage where *Gilligan* was shot. It was converted to a three-camera live stage. I still found sand in the corners, though. During this time I realized how lucky I had been to have had Max and Sherwood. They were two in a million. The ability to create, write, and produce full-time is a rare thing. (*The Good Guys* had Leonard Stern of *Get Smart* and Jerry Belson of *That Girl* as executive producers.)

We shot two shows on Friday night. To prove a point, I asked the network to let us charge the first audience five bucks. We'd give it back after the show. Then, let the second audience in free, as usual. I said the difference would be self-explanatory. They told me to forget it and never, never to bring it up again. They knew. The worst part of the whole experience was that after the last audience left, we stayed shooting "pick-ups" until two in the morning. Pick-ups are parts of a scene. The only problem was, we did pick-ups that ended up in reshooting the whole show. Then to top it off, they sweetened the laugh track with recorded laughs. What were we doing? Rehearse all week, shoot two live shows, then do it all over again. Madness.

I think it was during all this writing and rewriting that I first heard the expression "You can't polish a turd." A good script is hard to come by. We'd read the script on Monday, and on Tuesday we would have a brand-new script. Same Wednesday and Thursday. By Friday, at four P.M., the rewrites were still going on. Also during the pick-ups. With Max and Sherwood, I was used to shooting finished scripts. But enough moaning and groaning. Working with Herb and Joyce was the fun part. I'm sorry it wasn't a hit for them. Herb was a very funny man. Very creative. It was sad to see him wasted on this series. Same goes for Joyce.

There's no sense going through the series episode by episode, but we did a few that stand out. One was when Herb, as the owner of a diner, was cooking hamburgers on the grill. He was supposed to flip the patty into the air and it wouldn't come down for five beats. A propman was on the catwalk over the grill, with a butterfly net, so he could catch the burger. I was standing next to Herb when he flipped it up into the air. Only he didn't flip it up. He fired it at supersonic speed past the propman, over the set, and out of sight. The audience howled. Another try, and this one hit the wall behind us. The propman said to just give him a matching patty and he would drop it down no matter where Herb flipped his. The studio cats that roamed around the stages after everyone went home had a feast that night.

As a late-sixties series, we wanted to do a script that had some contemporary values to it. The network was leery of doing anything like that. In the second year we finally wore them down. Joyce, as Herb's wife, wants to beautify the roads by planting wildflowers along them. She puts the seeds in

capsules that are biodegradable and throws them out of the car as they drive along. The two are arrested for trying to grow marijuana. When asked if there are any more gang members, Herb says there's only one and he's back at the diner making hash. So I get busted, too. It was a pretty daring script for the time. And it was the only one we shot that was like that.

The irony of this series was that I had finally realized how to negotiate a good deal. I was to receive profit participation, or points, as they're called. Every time the series was rerun, I would collect. So far, it has been in limited runs in South America. No money. But who knows, maybe someday it will pay off.

One good thing came out of this mess. I was asked to replace Woody Allen on Broadway. He was finishing up a year's run in *Play It Again, Sam*. I thought, "Wow. I get to meet Woody Allen." I did and it was brief. I went to his dressing room on the last night. He mumbled a hello and was out the door. I found the Broadway audiences were the same as the audiences I played for around the country. That was because they were from all around the country. The *New York Times* reviewer came to a Wednesday matinee. In his review, he said he had never heard of *Gilligan's Island* but that I did an okay job.

When the run was over, I went to Tahiti, Bora-Bora, England, and Scotland. I was free, free at last!

MISCELLANEOUS MOVIES, TV APPEARANCES, AND PILOTS

Right after I got the part of Maynard I got to make my first movie. It was one of those B films that the Fox studio used to churn out in the late fifties, called *A Private Affair*. The plot centered around the high jinks of bunch of soldiers. It starred Sal Mineo, one of Bing Crosby's sons (I could never get them straight), and all the actors under contract to the studio. It may not have been an Oscar contender, but I was thrilled to be in a motion picture. I only had a few scenes, but one of them was with Jim Backus. He played a visiting senator with all the bluster and pompousness necessary and asked me about army life. When I reminded him about it five years later when we were shooting *Gilligan*, he looked at me and said, "That was you?" I knew he didn't remember doing the scene with me. It was just another forgettable movie for Jim.

The next movie the studio put me in was *Take Her, She's Mine*. It starred Jimmy Stewart and Sandra Dee. I played a beatnik. By this time the whole country knew me as Maynard G. Krebs, so this was a safe bit of typecasting. I

In *For Those Who Think Young* I got to practice yoga with Nancy Sinatra!

had a scene with Mr. Stewart in a coffeehouse. Talk about being nervous. We ran the lines a few times and then shot it. I had wondered if he would do his normal delivery with the *ahs* and *ums*. He did. I managed to get my words out and it was over too fast. I thought I had finally arrived on the show biz scene.

Later I did a "beach" movie in the early sixties called *For Those Who Think Young*. It starred James Darren and Nancy Sinatra. I played Jimmy's sidekick. The director wanted me to have a full beard for the part, so I grew one. I didn't know why until later.

Tina Louise was in the film, too. I didn't have any scenes with her. Never met her. Never even saw her. She doesn't list this film in her credits, but then, she won't say *Gilligan's Island* out loud either.

One day in the second week of shooting, when I walked on the stage, the assistant director asked why I was there. He said they were waiting for me on the scoring stage to record my song. I laughed at his joke and kept going. He grabbed me and said, "I'm not kidding. Jerry Fielding, who wrote all the music for this movie, a full orchestra, and backup singers are waiting. You're late!" I still thought he was putting me on. All this was news to me. Then he said, "Where's the sheet music for your song? You were supposed to get it two weeks ago. Wait here. I'll go get it for you." I thought, "What the hell is going on!" He came back and handed me my song on that sheet music that unfolds like an accordion. "Get going!" he said.

I walked across the lot in a daze, staring at all those notes and words. Maybe this was a bad dream. Nope. When I went into the scoring stage, there was Mr. Fielding standing on a podium with a baton, waiting. And there was the orchestra, and yup, there were the backup singers. I walked up to Mr. Fielding and he said, "Well, I see you have your music. What we'll do is rehearse it a couple of times and then record it." I said, "I don't think so. We have a slight problem." I explained the problem, and without blinking an eye he said, "No problem. We'll do the song a little piece at a time." We did. Not quite note by note, but close. It took all day. If there was an Academy Award for patience, Jerry Fielding should win.

In the movie I sang at the beach buried in the sand. Well, not completely buried. My chin and mouth stuck out. Two eyes and a nose were drawn upside down on my chin. It was photographed upside down so that my goatee became the little face's hair and my mustache the goatee. Sound confusing? How about lying with your head wrapped in towels, in a hole, covered with sand, and trying to lip-synch the song? I remember a muffled voice telling me I was off and I thought, "Everything's upside down. How can they tell if my lips match or not!" After many takes we got the song. I learned from this experience that you can't swallow up.

In *Have You Heard the One About the Traveling Saleslady* I costarred with Phyllis Diller. She is a funny lady, with one of the best laughs in the business. I played an inventor who lived on a farm. During one scene, one of the cows pooped. Phyllis looked down and said, "I'll never eat spinach soufflé again!" She was great to work with.

Who's Minding the Mint starred Jim Hutton, Dorothy Provine, Walter Brennan, Milton Berle, and Joey Bishop. I played a Good Humor man. It was directed by Howie Morris of Sid Caeser fame. We were shooting at two A.M. when Milton and Joey got into it. The scene called for all of us to drive our vehicles (including my ice cream truck) into the middle of this square, get out, and get in a group. Not too difficult, huh? Our director was up on a huge crane, high above the street. On action, I drove the truck into the square, jumped out, and joined Jim, Walter, Milton, and Joey in the middle of the street. I see Milton and Joey start to shove each other and hear their yelling. Poor Howie is trying to get off the crane and stop them. He finally gets to us and asks, what's the matter? The problem  seems to be over who was standing on whose mark. Howie explains that there are no marks because it's a very long shot. To him everybody is the size of an ant. One of the combatants says, "Well, there should be marks!" Howie finds a tiny piece of rope in the gutter and puts it down on the street. He goes back to the crane and is hoisted away. During the next take Milton and Joey fight over the piece of rope, each claiming it's his mark. Howie finally writes each one's name in chalk on the street, as Walter and I sit on the curb and watch.

In *Sweet Ride* I played a jazz-piano man. A straight part. It starred Tony Franciosa, Michael Sarrazin, and Jacqueline Bisset. We shot most of it at a beach house above Malibu. What a treat. One scene had me stoned and noodling some jazz on the piano. My stand-in was a jazz pianist, and I was going to have him play the real music for the scene. For the heck of it he taught me a few chords to rehearse with. In the take I played them and they used that version. Luckily, I was supposed to be high.

There was a motorcycle gang in the picture which was too real for its own good. They were a scary bunch. One lunchtime we all went to eat at a Mexican restaurant down from the studio. As I drove out the gate, I saw a police car pull a screeching U-turn and roar off down the street. When I arrived at the

Willie Owens, the ice cream man, in *Who's nding the Mint?*

(Overleaf) Phyllis Diller, me, and lots of cows in *Did You Hear the One About the Traveling Saleslady?*

157

Mexican restaurant, black-and-whites were all over the place. The "motorcycle gang" was lined up on the sidewalk surrounded by very nervous policemen. No guns were drawn, but hands were hovering. One by one the gang showed their SAG cards and were allowed to go into the restaurant. I don't think the employees got the word. The service was very fast and it was one of the quickest lunches I ever had.

In *Back to the Beach* I played a bartender who, I think, looked awfully like Gilligan. I'm not sure. The movie starred Frankie Avalon and Annette Funicello. In one scene I tell them that I knew this guy once who could build a nuclear reactor out of a couple of pineapples and a coconut, but he couldn't build a boat! I hope Russell saw that one!

When I wasn't working on a series, I appeared on lots of TV shows.

Perry Como was really the most relaxed man I ever worked with. He took a nap a half hour before airtime, and this was a live show. He'd wake up five minutes before his opening entrance and take an elevator down to the stage from his dressing room. He had it timed so that he casually walked from the elevator, around the back of the set, onto the stage, and started singing, "Dream along with me," etc.

During a Pat Boone special I received a pair of white buckskin shoes.

On an *I Dream of Jeannie* episode I played the klutzy son of the head genie. I fell down a chimney instead of into the lagoon! Working with Larry Hagman was a blast. He's one of the best physical comedians I know. I appeared on a mess of *Love Boat*s. In one I had to wear an evening dress. Markie Post

In *The Invisible Woman* with Alexa Hamilton I play a biochemist. Talk about typecasting!

ook at this TV nostalgia
erload! *High School USA*
ted stars from such hit
ows as *Leave It to Beaver*
ony Dow), *Dobie Gillis*
wayne Hickman), *Family*
es (Michael J. Fox),
'ligan's Island (me), and
ther Knows Best (Elinor
nahue). This show also
arred the very eccentric
ispin Glover.

wore one, too. Nobody had any trouble telling us apart. I took a trip to Acapulco on one with my darling wife, Dreama. When we arrived back in Los Angeles, she didn't want to get off the boat. She wanted to know where it was going next.

On *The Andy Griffith Show* I played a hillbilly, what else?

In the TV movie *High School U.S.A.*, starring Michael J. Fox, I played the father of Crispin Glover. (What a character!) Crispin played Michael J. Fox's father in *Back to the Future*. Mr. Fox is as nice as you think he is.

I also appeared in the pilot *The Invisible Woman*. It starred Alexa Hamilton, David Doyle, Ron Pallilo, Harvey Korman, and George Gobel. I was the scientist who developed the solution that made my niece invisible. Harvey Korman went into a mud pit, not me. Hooray!

In *Scamps*, a pilot, I starred with my wife, Dreama, and nine kids under the age of nine. I was a writer who worked at home and took care of the kids after school. The star of the show was really Joey Lawrence, who was five and three-quarters years of age. He was a natural-born actor. Recently, he's been on the TV show *Blossom* and is a big recording star now. Way to go, Joey! I knew you'd go on to bigger and better things.

And there was more Gilligan over the years. In the 1970s, I did the voice on two animated series: *The New Adventures of Gilligan* and *Gilligan's Planet*. All the old cast—except Tina Louise—did their character's voices as well. And in 1988 I turned up as Gilligan on *ALF* and again in 1991 on *Baywatch*.

In spring 1993, I turned up as the high school graduation speaker on *Evening Shade*. The gag was that they actually wanted *John* Denver but somebody goofed.

The real stars of *Scamps*, Joey Lawrence and my wife, Dreama.

Scamps, with nine kids under nine. What did say about working with kids and anim

THE *GILLIGAN* MOVIES

RESCUE FROM GILLIGAN'S ISLAND

The first TV movie was *Rescue From Gilligan's Island*. The castaways finally get off the island and return to civilization. We shot it in 1978, fifteen years after *Gilligan* went on the air. Mothers all over the country asked me in those years to please make a show where we were rescued. They said that every time they had to take their children to any kind of appointment—doctor, dentist, etc.—the kids would always scream and cry that they were going to miss the episode when we got rescued. I thought it would get a big rating. It did, and because of that high rating, a 52 share, we got to make two more.

For *Rescue* we went right back to the old lagoon. It was the same. On the first day, after two hours of shooting, it was as if the fifteen years had not happened. An art director who had been on location for two months was walking to his office when he happened to glance down at the lagoon. A friend who was with him told me later that the director didn't say a word. He just went to his office, picked up the phone, and asked in a quavering voice if *Gilligan* was shooting on the lot. "Thank God," he said. "I thought for a minute there I had lost it!"

Tina declined to make an appearance. Either they wouldn't pay her enough, or she was afraid it might ruin her dramatic acting career. She never really liked the series, and after being typecast as Ginger, she liked it even less. If that was possible. The rest of us had a ball.

The scene when we arrived back in civilization was shot at Marina del Rey in L.A., not Honolulu. There were fireboats shooting geysers of water into the air, coast guard cutters were whooping, and all kinds of pleasure boats sur-rounded our hut-boat. People came out of the restaurants and bars lining the harbor just to see what was going on. I could imagine some drunk at a bar looking out the window and seeing us go by. He probably joined AA on the spot.

We shot at the marina for a week or so, and I played a joke on the prop man that kind of backfired. All during the show, I had to wear a medallion on a leather thong around my neck. It was essential to the plot. For some reason, props only had one medallion and another that could only be used in long shots. Usually, they'd have a dozen or so. I asked the assistant propman to get me the second one and I switched them. I pretended to become frustrated and angry over some line I had and took off the medallion, twirled it, and threw it into the water. The propman ran to the edge of the dock, did some quick triangulation, and took off to hire some scuba divers. All before I could stop

Rescue and *Castaway on Gilligan's Island* brou
the whole gang together again, except Tina v
was replaced by Judith Baldv

him. He came back with the divers and I showed him the real medallion I'd had in my pocket. He glanced at it and then started telling the divers where he thought the location was for them to dive. I grabbed his arm and said, "Look, here it is!" He did a double take and didn't laugh. I knew I was in real trouble for the rest of the movie.

That medallion caused more trouble than it was worth. We were shooting onstage and an actor had flown in from N.Y. to play one part. We had shot three scenes; he was dismissed and left. He was flying right back to N.Y. Then my dear wife, Dreama, said to me, between setups, "Honey, aren't you supposed to be wearing the medallion?" Nobody—and that includes the director, the script girl, props, the actors, Sherwood, and me—had noticed that I wasn't wearing it. They stopped the N.Y. actor at the gate and got him back. We had to shoot all the scenes again. Dreama had saved the company anywhere between fifty and a hundred thousand dollars. If she hadn't noticed I didn't have the medallion on, they would have had to fly the actor back from N.Y., rent the studio again, and basically reshoot everything. I thought she should get a cash reward or at least a gift for her acute observation. She received a thank-you. That's show, without the biz.

Alan and I were in the water a lot. The best time we had was in the tank during the shark scenes. Gilligan's fishing and hooks a shark, which pulls him through the water. The Skipper jumps in, grabs him, and the two of them get towed through the water. Then the Professor grabs the Skipper and now there are three. Since Alan was holding on to my waist as we plowed along, he could lift me, so my head was out of the water, or he could push down and under I'd go. He was having a great time. It took about two hours to shoot this scene, and at the start of one of the pulls, I heard Alan shouting behind me, "This is better than Disneyland! It's an E ride for sure!" I started laughing and almost drowned. He lifted me up as we skimmed along and said, "What's the matter, little buddy, can't take a joke!" and roared.

We were shooting at the lagoon at around five in the afternoon in November. It was cold and windy. The last shot of the day was to be all of us in the lagoon. We decided among ourselves to keep putting off the shot, until it got

...cue From Gilligan's Island—a reunion. Is that my
...cream cone the Skipper has his eye on?

169

too dark to shoot. We could do it the next day when it was warmer. When the director tried to round up the cast, at least one was always missing. We had almost made it when we heard a voice from the lagoon calling to us: "Come on in! It's just like the pool in my backyard." It was Natalie, treading water, feather hat and all. Nobody had told her the plan. Alan and I looked at each other and I said to him, "Please, just pick me up and throw me in." He did.

At the end of the movie, the Skipper and Gilligan have a new boat, the *Minnow II*. They invite the former passengers to go for a little sail with them, and the dummies accept. How stupid can you be? A storm arises and it's back on Gilligan's Island again.

Dawn has not lost her "girl next door" cha

THE CASTAWAYS ON GILLIGAN'S ISLAND

Gilligan finds an old World War Two plane and the Professor says he can fix it up and make it fly. Sure he can fix a, ah, never mind. He fixes the plane and they fly off the island. An engine quits and they're forced to return. They're rescued after the plane showed up on radar. Howell builds a hotel on the island. This was a real attempt at a pilot for a series. It was *Love Boat, Fantasy Island,* and *Hotel,* all rolled into one. The network decided to break it into two one-hour segments and show them a week apart. The ratings went through the cellar. No one had any hope it would go to series. Again Tina didn't play Ginger. I think she got more press that way.

THE HARLEM GLOBETROTTERS ON GILLIGAN'S ISLAND

The third and last TV movie got messed up from the start. It was written with Howell carrying the whole plot. It was his story, but Jim was too ill to do it. At the last minute David Ruprecht was signed to play his son. (I never knew the Howells had a son.) David did a great job. The Harlem Globetrotters had many scenes with a great deal of dialogue. They were much better basketball players than actors. They were always up, even at two in the morning. I asked them, how come? They said that they traveled the world as America's ambassadors, and one of the rules was to be always friendly and happy. They were. In one small country, where the people had never seen blacks before, they couldn't understand how there were racial problems in this country. After all, these guys were six foot eight or over.

I found myself asking the Globetrotters for autographs on a basketball and trading my hat for a jersey. They were a good childhood memory, as is *Gilligan's Island,* and I understood why people asked me for my autograph. When you look back at when you were a kid and something you remember makes you smile, it's almost impossible not to ask for an autograph. In all the years I've signed them, not one person has been rude or negative. What I hear a lot is, ''I ran home from school every day to watch your show.'' One mother of a four-year-old girl told me her daughter always came in from playing outside at four in the afternoon to watch the show. The mom asked her how she knew it was on, since she couldn't tell time. She said that when the sun touched the top of the big tree, she knew it was time for *Giggle'ns Island.*

My wife Dreama played the Howell's social secretary. She was cute and gorgeous in the part. It was really fun to have her working with me. She's the best. We're married seventeen years and it just gets better and better. Lucky me!

How far can you push a TV concept? *The Ha Globetrotters on Gilligan's Island.* I'm flanke guest castaways Barbara Bain and Martin Lan

Chuck McCann and I shared the cartoon-like antics on *Far Out Space Nuts*, which ran for sixteen Saturday morning episodes.

SYNDICATED SERIES

FAR OUT SPACE NUTS

There were only sixteen episodes of *Far Out Space Nuts*. It was for Saturday morning to replace a cartoon with live actors. The difference was minimal. It was shot on tape and the director stayed in the control room and gave suggestions over a speaker. When we (Chuck McCann and I) couldn't understand them, he would run down to the set, explain them, and run back up to the control room. Most of the time, we still didn't understand them. We had monsters from outer space on almost every show. It was a real cheap *Star Trek*. Some very good actors played monsters. I was especially embarrassed for one. John Carradine was covered in blue makeup and then sprinkled with glitter. Here was an actor with a career that spanned generations. Major films to his credit. A classic actor in every sense of the word. In the first scene he had a long speech. When he was done, I just stood there. His pronunciation, his deep voice, his presence, the way the words came tripping off his tongue, left me speechless. I was waiting for more. Mesmerized was what I was. The speaker on the wall yelled "Cut!" and John smiled at me. I guess he had seen this type of reaction before. On take two, I got my lines out and I realized I was still just a beginner. Had a long way to go. I guess part of the old adage "There are no small parts" is true.

My youngest daughter, Emily (she was two then), used to sleep on a mattress on the set. When I took her to lunch her favorite thing was to put black olives on all her fingers and wiggle them, then eat them one by one.

DUSTY'S TRAIL

Dusty's Trail was created and produced by Sherwood. It was *Gilligan's Island* in the West. Forrest Tucker as the wagon master (Skipper), Dusty as the guide (Gilligan), a rich couple in a stagecoach (Mr. and Mrs. Howell), a saloon girl (Ginger), a schoolteacher (Mary Ann), and an engineer (Professor). The premise was that Dusty could never find the West. The wagon train wandered all over the place. I had always wanted to do a western just so I could shoot myself in the foot. I got what I wanted. More than a few times.

We did twenty-six episodes, and the later ones are kind of blurred for me. We did two a week, finishing one at noon Wednesday and starting the next one right after lunch, at one P.M. It wasn't like it was a word comedy; we had horses, lots of horses, a stagecoach, and a covered wagon. My horse had more movie credits than I did. He also had more energy. He'd come to the set at seven-thirty in the morning raring to go. I asked the wranglers what they

Dusty's Trail—working with Sherwood Schwartz again.

were doing to him. They said they were waking him up at six and then riding him till seven to get the edge off him. I said, don't wake him up until it's time to bring him to the set. Let him sleep to the last minute. I like sleepy horses. He had two gears: full gallop and a skidding stop. He could hit his mark every time. He moved when the director called action. He was mucho horse and I wasn't a macho rider.

We had a double soundstage at Twentieth Century-Fox that was filled with dirt, bushes, and trees. Sometimes we had to do run-bys. That meant that all of us had to ride by the camera in one shot. The stage wasn't big enough for

that, so the big doors at either end were opened. We'd gallop out one, ride around in front of the stage, then back in the other door. The studio had to stop all traffic on that part of the lot when this happened. I wish they had stopped the run-bys. Still, it was a sight to see. Out of one door came Forrest, then me, then the stagecoach, and then the covered wagon. By the time the covered wagon was out, Forrest and I were going back in, and of course by the time the covered wagon was going in, here came Forrest and me out again. People came from all over the lot to watch this spectacle.

We used some actors who couldn't ride. Why not? Neither could I. There was one scene where an actor jumps off his horse and is supposed to fire three shots. In the rehearsal, he pantomimed doing it next to the horse's head. Not a smart thing to do. The blanks we used left your ears ringing. The wranglers watched the scene and didn't say anything. Maybe I should say a word about the wranglers. They liked nothing better than playing jokes on the actors, but this was going too far. I went up to one and asked had he seen the scene. "Yup," he said. I asked him if he wasn't worried that the horse would probably react badly to this and run around wildly, destroying the set and maybe a few actors? "Nope," he said. On the take, the actor leapt off the horse and fired three booming shots next to its head. Nothing happened. I went over to the wrangler and asked him how he did that. With a small smile, he said, "Stone deaf." They had got me again.

When the series was over, it took me a month just to rest up. It ran briefly, was seen by few, and disappeared from the airwaves. It rests now in a vault somewhere. Peacefully, I hope, but it will probably be resurrected someday. That's all right; there were some pretty funny episodes.

WORKING ONSTAGE

From the early seventies to the mid-eighties, I traveled around the United States and Canada doing plays. In fact, I met my wife, Dreama, doing *Play It Again, Sam* in '77. Sometimes you get real lucky. We haven't been apart since. We did this play until I couldn't do it anymore. When a stage manager said he had a list of changes and they were ones I had made over the years, I knew it was time to retire. Dinner theaters were in their heyday then, opening and closing all over the place. This "art" form died in the eighties. (There are still many dinner theaters throughout the country, so I wouldn't say they actually died.) They were generally owned and run by people who knew nothing about theater or the restaurant business. Two of the most difficult to operate successfully. I had one go out from under me between the second and third acts. As I was doing the third act, I could see the employees at the back of the

mom (left), my niece Helen (right), and an
entified friend come to visit on the *Gilligan* set
ng a cowboy dream sequence.

theater taking everything that wasn't nailed down. They knew they weren't going to be paid. On the back wall was a large oil painting of me that I wanted, but I saw it go out the side door. If you are the one who took it and are reading this, I want it! I had to sit and pose for days.

The things that happen when you're in front of a theater audience are completely different from those that happen when you're filming. A man laughing so hard, he falls into the aisle and does ten minutes with the audience. People talking to you while you're in a scene. You hear sniggering laughter and you know your fly is open. The stories go on and on. Still, being onstage is the most rewarding thing for any actor, for many reasons.

I'm asked a lot what I'm doing now. Well, besides enjoying life with my beautiful wife and son Colin on a mountain in West Virginia, I go to L.A. to do various jobs. What takes most of my time is building my first Bob Denver's Putt-Putt, an indoor miniature golf course where you play eighteen holes in a jungle. No headhunters. A hole in one on eighteen makes the volcano erupt. All proceeds will go to the handicapped where the Putt-Putt is located. I hope to get the first one built this fall. Maybe you'll have one in your town real soon. Until then, keep smiling.

My wife Dreama and I when we were making the dinner-theater circuit.

I am onstage in *Murder at Howard Johnson's*.